LIGHTHOUSES
OF THE ATLANTIC

À mon père,
« Merci de m'avoir ouvert les yeux sur la mer. »
PHILIP PLISSON

The old carbide lamp at the Ar-Men lighthouse in France. When first developed in 1881, it was considered a great leap in technology. Today it is a museum piece.

LIGHTHOUSES
OF THE ATLANTIC

PHOTOGRAPHY BY
PHILIP PLISSON⚓ AND GUILLAUME PLISSON

TEXT BY
DANIEL CHARLES

CASSELL&CO

Lighthouse country

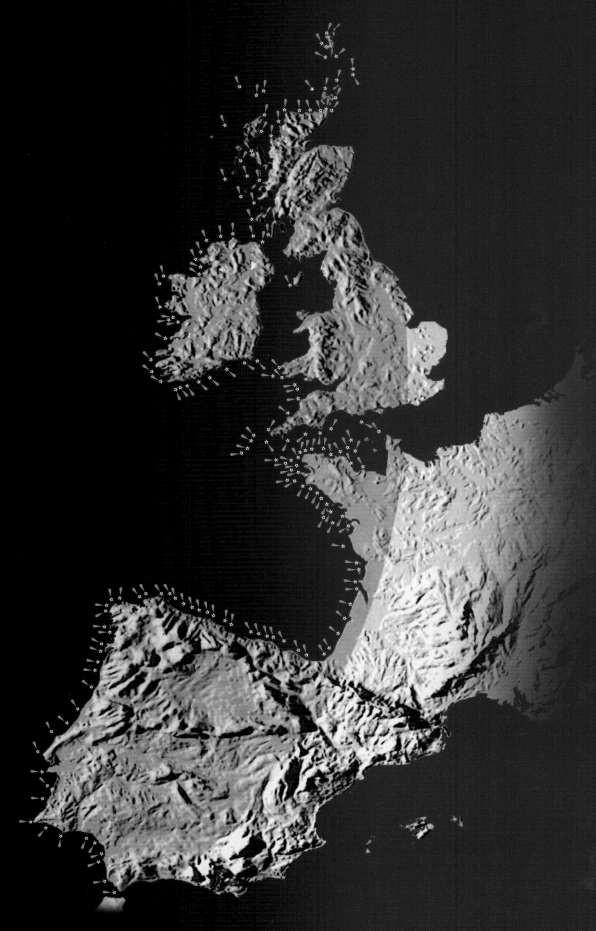

A lighthouse is not just a light on the horizon; it is far more than a tower, a silvery beam of light in the night sky, an isolated watchman. For the sailor, each one is unique: the flashing lights or the foghorn signal landfall, of course, but also instantly let ships know exactly where they are: Eddystone in Cornwall, La Jument in France or Torre de Hercules in Spain. Some send out beams of green or red warning lights, visible only from a certain portion of the sea, warning captains that they may be in treacherous waters if they are able to see one light or the other. In areas with heavy fog, foghorns are far more important than the lights. Ardnamurchan in Scotland is a good place to appreciate the range of a foghorn, which can be the size of a small bus. A lighthouse can send messages in Morse code or light up a radar screen. It is a unique type of maritime structure, a building that can withstand hell and high water and remain resolutely upright unlike most industrial constructions that lie flat across the land. A lighthouse is far more than a tower, more than a shaft of light in the night sky. The very nature of a lighthouse is to stand out: by its height, cost, technical complexity, complex construction techniques, isolation and spectacular appearance.

Left

The lantern of the Cordouan lighthouse, surrounded by the sea, waves and wind.

The Tuskar lighthouse, in Ireland.

Iₜ's hardly surprising that lighthouses have captured the human imagination. These nearly mythical buildings are rich in symbolism: for the engineer, the lighthouse represents the ultimate in daring and imagination; for the philosopher, a metaphor for knowledge shedding its light on the world; for the optician, a marvellous application of his science; and finally, for the sailor, it's a ray of hope, the first hint of a port of call. For the last two hundred years, lighthouses have fired the imagination of novelists, from Jules Verne's work, *The Lighthouse at the End of the World* to Rachilde's erotic book, *The Lighthouse of Love.* Yet fiction pales before reality: even in the realm of the incredible, lighthouses have impressive tales to tell, such as "The man who swallowed molten lead" or "The mysterious disappearance of the Flannan Island keepers," stories worthy of Sherlock Holmes, with the difference that these happen to be true.

The very nature of a lighthouse is to stand out: by its height, cost, technical complexity, complex construction techniques, isolation and spectacular appearance.

Another word for a lighthouse or beacon is *pharos*, after the island of Pharos in the Bay of Alexandria, which was the site of the world's first lighthouse.[1] One of the Seven Wonders of the World, the lighthouse was over 110 metres (361 feet) high, making it the tallest lighthouse ever. The Greek architect Sostratus of Cnidos built it in the third century BC. Yet the science of lighthouses did not develop in the Mediterranean: the techniques necessary to build the world's most solid towers were developed in a tougher, more rugged and formative environment: Europe's Atlantic coast, which stretches 2,800 kilometres (1,740 miles) from the Shetlands to Gibraltar.

The Ardnamurchan foghorn.

The Lusitanians (who lived in the region that would later become Portugal) travelled far afield, sailing as far as Ireland. They brought with them two important things: their writing the ogham alphabet was used there until the end of the pre-Christian era and the Christian faith, which the Irish exported to the north of Scotland and beyond (as far as America, according to the fifth-century legend of Saint Brendan). Cork was one of the most important ports in the Middle Ages. Wines from Portugal and the Aquitaine region, as well as indigo from Toulouse, were traded there for pewter and slate from Wales and Scotland. Soon after, the sea route to America was opened (Portuguese fishermen and merchants from Bristol played a major role, even if Columbus received all the credit). By the sixteenth century, the Atlantic coast was a beacon that heralded Europe to returning sailors.

It was, however, extraordinarily difficult to get back to the Old Continent, with its rocky shores defended by treacherous reefs known to sailors simply as "hazards". The coasts needed to be lit with fires and beacons, and lighthouses had to be built. The history of lighthouses was written here, and the entire Atlantic coast is like a living museum. The Torre de Hercules (the Tower of Hercules), the world's oldest working lighthouse, has signalled La Coruña in Spain since the second century. Cordouan, the first modern lighthouse, was positioned at the mouth of the Gironde in France in 1611; in 1823, it was the first beacon to be equipped with the revolutionary optics invented by Augustin Fresnel. The third Eddystone lighthouse (1759) finally established the techniques for building lighthouses on the open sea. Ar-Men (1881) was the most difficult to build: it took fourteen years. And so it went—up to Rathlin O'Birne, in Ireland, the only lighthouse in the world with its own source of nuclear energy.

This arc of lights is divided into six zones: Scotland, from the Shetlands to the Isle of Man, and the Atlantic coasts of Ireland, England, France, Spain and Portugal. Each country and region has left its mark on its lighthouses, yet these shining sentinels are not so much national standard-bearers as the fruit of European exchange. Ar-Men was built using techniques perfected by the Englishman John Smeaton and the Scot Alan Stevenson, while Skerryvore, Stevenson's masterpiece, was lit by optics made in France. Until recently, the lens invented by Augustin Fresnel was used in lighthouses all over the world, and Spanish and Portuguese lighthouses were lit by Barbier, Bénard and Turenne in Paris, or the Anciens Etablissements Harlé, while the Chance Brothers of Birmingham supplied lights to Ireland. The Atlantic coast was an area of intense exchange. This European outpost was a nation in its own right: lighthouse country.

The science of lighthouses and signal lights is called "pharology", after the island of Pharos in the Bay of Alexandria, site of the ancient world's most famous lighthouse.

Seafarers of the past had no maps (or such as they had were so inaccurate as to be practically worthless) and no means of calculating their position. In bad weather, they made their way forward by dead reckoning and often depended on little more than good luck. Monks during the Crusades drew up the first handwritten navigational documents; these included lists of capes, noteworthy places and recommended routes, like early pilot books. Christianity had linked the various posts of the Atlantic coast: now it helped sailors cross it. Monks lighted the earliest beacons, because saving sailors' lives meant that they would one day probably die on Christian soil, with their souls saved. As early as the fifth century, the monks of Saint Dubhan lit fires at the south-east tip of Catholic Ireland, not far from Cork, on the spot where the black and white tower of Hook Head now stands. Another Irish beacon was lit in 1190 in Youghal; it was kept alight by nuns from the convent of Saint Anne. In France, at the end of the fifteenth century, a hermit lit a fire at the top of the tower of Cordouan, erected by the Black Prince.[2] Monks built the first three Portuguese lights—on the Douro, at São Vicente and Cascais. And even when the flames weren't directly ecclesiastical, they had their origins in religion: in 1314, Walter de Godeton, a member of a small community of wreckers at Saint Catherine, on the Isle of Wight, plundered some barrels of wine from a wreck. All would have been well—if the wine had not been intended for the Church. The sinner found himself threatened with excommunication, and, as penance for his love of altar wine, was made to finance the construction of a lighthouse, which his family then maintained for two hundred years.

Thanks to the beacons lit by monks, the sight of a fire became associated with a safe haven, but the unscrupulous took advantage of this to light false beacons, sending passing ships straight onto sharp rocks. From the late Middle Ages until the early nineteenth century, thriving communities of wreckers picked off ships like vultures. One Welsh wrecker used to attach a lantern to a donkey's tail, which swayed like a signal when the animal moved. Retribution did, however, occur: the bishop of Aberbrothock installed a warning bell on Bell Rock, which was removed by a pirate—who is said to have been shipwrecked on the very same reef when he didn't see it in time.

Around 1215, a brotherhood was created at the instigation of the bishop of Canterbury. It consisted of "God-fearing men who promise, in the love of Christ the Lord and in the name of the masters and members of the guild of The Trinity, to suppress those whom the Devil induces to lead ships to their destruction with false lights ... by building and lighting beacons to guide sailors." Other "Trinity Houses" were created (nearly eight centuries later, the British lighthouse and pilot authority is still called Trinity House). There were guilds in Dover, Dundee, Hull, Leith (Edinburgh), London and Newcastle. There were none in France, Spain or Portugal. The sailors of those countries put their trust in God, but British merchants preferred more secular guarantees. In 1261, the barons of the port of Winchelsea (on the south coast of England) were licensed to collect the sum of twopence for every ship that came into the port, in exchange for the upkeep of the lighthouse. The fee had not changed three hundred years later, when the Newcastle Trinity House was commissioned to build two lighthouses on the Tyne estuary and was entitled to collect twopence per boat (fourpence for foreigners). It was a small sum—fourteen times less, for example, than the tax on a pint of whisky some years later—but its impact was enormous: it created two distinct policies toward lighthouse management on the Atlantic coast, a division that would last for almost three hundred years.

Everyone agreed that ships should be taxed according to their tonnage; the resulting funds were used to develop ports, levy armies and so on. The two schools of thought

The interior of a medieval lighthouse (Hook Head, Ireland).

concerning lighthouses, however, separated the north from the south. In the south, it was taken for granted that sailors should not have to pay for their safety, which is still the case in France today. Lighthouses were everybody's responsibility—and therefore nobody's. So the coasts remained in darkness, except for a few lights built by monks and the Cordouan lighthouse, erected through the generosity of a private donor. In the north, on the other hand, religious initiatives were all the more unlikely as British monasteries had been dissolved in 1560. Successive sovereigns, lacking state funds, entrusted lighthouses to private individuals who were responsible for building them, seeing to their upkeep and collecting a toll ("light-dues") from each passing ship. The financing of lighthouses became independent of central government, and these towers, built in the most desolate outposts of the British Isles, became extraordinary sources of wealth. It was more profitable to own a lighthouse on a well-travelled reef than a string of buildings in London. For an equivalent surface area, no other human activity was as profitable as a lighthouse. During the first half of the nineteenth century, a lighthouse made a net profit of from £3,000 to £20,000—at a time when a worker lived on less than £100 per annum. There was even a one-time wrecker who converted and became a lighthouse owner: it was better business and far less risky. The prospect of these huge profits year after year whetted appetites and fostered a certain level of official corruption. There was a considerable advantage, however, in this situation: however costly it might be to build a lighthouse, it was guaranteed to be profitable. The time was ripe for Great Britain to become the site of the first lighthouses constructed in impossible locations. The first of these was Eddystone.

God-fearing men who promise, in the love
of Christ the Lord and in the name of the masters
and brethren of the guild of The Trinity, to suppress
those whom the Devil induces to lead ships
to their destruction with false lights...
by building and lighting beacons to guide sailors.

The Trinity House coat of arms.

Before exploring this legendary lighthouse, it might be useful to examine these "sentries of light," as Victor Hugo called them, from another angle. Lighthouses may be built to last, but they do evolve. As sailors' expectations and technical expertise evolved, new lighthouses were built, or old ones were equipped with new lenses. The story of the Cordouan lighthouse is exemplary: its light first shone around 1495; then from 1584 to 1611, it was reconstructed by Louis de Foix in an extraordinarily Baroque style. In 1789, Teulère demolished the third floor and raised the height of the whole thing, giving the lighthouse its present appearance, and installed the reflector that he thought he had invented (but which others had actually thought of before him). In 1823, Fresnel set up his first lens there, and in 1862, Cordouan was the first building to be listed, with Notre-Dame, as a French Historic Monument. The lighthouse was finally equipped with electricity in 1948.

Eddystone is another such example. Four lighthouses have been constructed on the site, from Eddystone I to Eddystone IV. Statistics, records and measurements are inseparable from lighthouse construction. A lighthouse has the supreme simplicity of a number. An official hierarchy classifies lighthouses in order from one to six,[3] according to visibility—but this classification tells us little about the true class of the towers or of their social standing among the waves. Just like land constructions, some are noble, others less so. The latter may rise above inaccessible capes and cling to cliffs too steep for goats, but in pharology, the study of lighthouses, the criterion of nobility is difficulty, lack of comfort. Noble lighthouses stand in the sea with every high tide, and their lanterns are lost in the mist

The Cordouan light sends out its beam, as it has done every evening for the last six hundred years.

La Jument.

during each storm. These towers are anchored onto reefs and battered by the waves; these lighthouses on rocks include Ar-Men, La Jument, Skerryvore, Chicken Rock and Fastnet Rock. And of all these solitary barons, one stands out above all the rest: Eddystone, the father of them all.

Every technical advance is the result of trial and error: for pharologists, the major advances occurred on a series of reefs some fifty degrees north of the Equator, a little more than four degrees west of the Greenwich meridian, and right in the middle of the Atlantic coast. Incidentally, this reef, fourteen miles from Plymouth, is one of the most improbable intersections in the world: this wave-battered rock played its part in the history of lighthouses, walls, swimming pools and toilets.

The Eddystone reefs had claimed thousands of lives and destroyed many a ship's cargo. This situation was most unfavourable to the nearby port of Plymouth and had to be rectified. In 1664, the Admiralty expressed its concern in no uncertain terms, but someone had to be found to undertake the construction of a lighthouse. Trinity House spent thirty years looking for a contractor, only to have him back out at the last minute: the task seemed impossible. But that was before Henry Winstanley came forward. An inventor, he had invented a sophisticated plumbing system, consisting of a hygienic vase with a flush; he had demonstrated the latter in London before a rather bemused gathering. He believed he could build a lighthouse, and Trinity House granted him the future profits for five years, after which time they would share, fifty-fifty.

In 1696, Winstanley set to work as often as the sea would let him, but this was only in calm weather, and only once he had rowed fourteen miles to the reef (and back again). At this time, England and France were at war; one day, when the inventor and his team were working on the rock, they were taken prisoner by one of the king's corsairs. When they reached France, the pirate was flung into the Bastille and Winstanley was freed, with the following message from Louis XIV: "We are at war with England, not with humanity."

Difficulty and discomfort are the criteria for judging the nobility of a lighthouse. So the most majestic lighthouses stand in the sea with every high tide, and their lanterns are lost in the mist during each storm.

The Staircase of Honour at Trinity House, London.

kers camped in the unfinished building; once, during a storm, they were stranded there for eleven days. Eddystone I finally shone out on 14 November 1698. The bottom of the tower was made of stone and the top, 24.4 metres (80 feet) high, was wooden, but during the winter waves came crashing over the top of it. Winstanley was convinced that the structure was too weak, so the following year he increased the diameter by 170 percent, reinforced the stonework with metal rings and raised the tower to 36.58 metres (120 feet). Eddystone I (version 2) was inaugurated in October 1699. Its light went out for the last time on November 27, 1703. On that day, Winstanley had taken some workmen out to do urgent repairs. There was a hurricane, and the waves are said to have been up to 45 metres (148 feet) high. Eighty ships were sunk in the Channel alone, with five of these wrecks accounting for 1,124 dead. The first Eddystone lighthouse was swept out to sea, together with its occupants.

The lighthouse was reinforced during its construction and made higher than originally planned. To avoid the six-hour row from Plymouth every day, Winstanley and his workers camped in the unfinished building; once, during a

Conclusion: stonework, which had been perfect for the sheltered banks of Cordouan, was not strong enough to cling to such an exposed rock. Another technique had to be found. John Rudyerd, a silk merchant, considered that the late Winstanley's mistake had been to use a technique developed on dry land. The sea required another approach: the tower had to be built like a ship.

Europe's most powerful lighthouse:
Créac'h, at the tip of Brittany, visible from a distance of 66.5 km (41 miles)

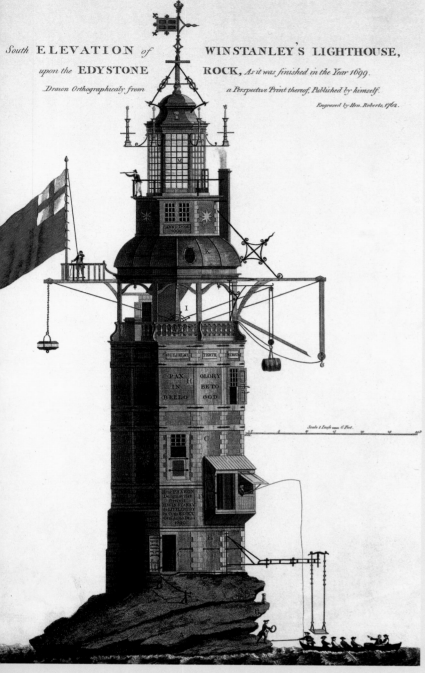

The first Eddystone lighthouse. It stood for four years, then was swept away, along with its inventor.

This time, the operation was financed by a certain Colonel Lovett, who negotiated a 99-year licence. In exchange for a rent of £100, he would keep all profits. John Rudyerd set to work, with the help of two naval carpenters. He designed a conical tower, the first of its kind: it would offer less resistance to the waves than a hexagonal construction. The rock was pierced by hand, granite blocks (hewed by hand) were bolted to, and oak frames (sawn by hand) were attached to these. Eddystone II's light first shone in 1709. It was a stationary vessel, 21.60 metres (71 feet) high. The tallest waves completely submerged it and the tower trembled, but it held tight. Lovett died in 1710, and Rudyerd in 1713, and the lighthouse acquired new owners—and new enemies: worms. For thirty years, the planks had to be replaced one by one, before they were eaten away. The work would have gone on even longer than 2 December 1755, but that night, an even more deadly enemy attacked the lighthouse: fire.

Eddystone II was lit by a central light that held several dozen tallow candles. In order for them to burn regularly, a keeper had to come and shorten the wicks every 30 minutes. At two o'clock in the morning, Henry Hall climbed up to cut the candlewicks. He was the head keeper, despite having reached the ripe old age of ninety-four. There was so much smoke in the lantern that when Hall opened the balcony door, the draught kindled the ashes, which set fire to the tallow that had accumulated on the walls over the past forty-six years. The old man tried to put the fire out by himself, while waiting for the other two keepers to arrive. They soon had to beat a retreat. They continued to throw buckets of water through the trap door (hatch) onto the lantern floor. The lead roof collapsed, and Hall cried: "I'm on fire! I've swallowed fire!" The others were too busy to take much notice of the old man, who, apart from his difficulties in speaking, didn't seem to be in too much pain. At last the heat forced them back. They took refuge at the foot of the lighthouse, where they were bombarded with burning debris and attacked by the waves. A small boat picked them up eight hours after the fire had started. Henry Hall was delirious and kept saying that he had swallowed molten lead. He died twelve days later. At the autopsy, a 207-gram (7-ounce) lead ingot was found in his stomach: this was all that remained of Eddystone II.

Everybody wanted an Eddystone III: the Admiralty, the port of Plymouth and the holders of this lucrative licence, which was valid until 1807. Problems remained, however: the first lighthouse had proved that usual building techniques were inadequate, while the second had demonstrated the inefficiency of naval construction. This time, the task was entrusted neither to a lavatory inventor nor a silk merchant, but to one of the first civil engineers, John Smeaton. He was convinced that man should imitate nature, as human techniques were inadequate. His idea was to extend the rock vertically upwards, like a tree. No lighthouse had yet been built in this way, but he was determined to try.

In 1992, the Musée de la Marine in Paris organised an exhibition[4] for children featuring the most beautiful lighthouses, built with Lego bricks. The models were extraordinarily realistic—perhaps because they were constructed according to the techniques used by Smeaton and his followers. The English engineer also used building blocks for Eddystone III, but in this case, the bricks were of granite, weighed several tons, and were hand-cut and shaped, each one bevelled to fit the others exactly. This work could obviously not be done on site, so it was carried out in Plymouth, where the stones were assembled into a tower, then taken apart again to be transported out to the reef. In other words, Eddystone III was the world's first entirely prefabricated building. To be certain that the blocks wouldn't move, Smeaton added marble wedges between the horizontal layers, and he cemented the blocks together. The mortar used in Smeaton's day was hardly more resistant than plaster, but, undeterred, he perfected a technique elaborated in Portland: he mixed and burned equal quantities of lime and chalk, creating Portland cement. This was the first modern cement, and it is still used on exterior walls, swimming-pool walls and so on.

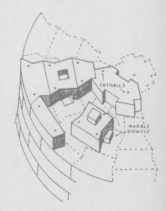

Enormous blocks of stone, shaped to dovetail together.

After all this preparatory work, things should have moved ahead swiftly—but the rock was isolated and working conditions were atrocious. The first two-ton block was set in place on 12 June 1757, but the new light-house was only inaugurated twenty-eight months and sixteen thousand pounds later (the owners were compensated, however, by an annual profit of over five thousand pounds). Smeaton wrote a "Narrative of the Construction of the Eddystone Lighthouse", in which he recounted every detail of the venture: this was the first major reference work for lighthouse builders (although its author complained that the book gave him more trouble than the lighthouse). In 1882, Eddystone III was replaced by Eddystone IV, for reasons which will be explained in the chapter on English lighthouses. Other lighthouses were built on even more difficult rocks—but the technique perfected by Smeaton was used practically unchanged for two hundred years.

Of course, other sorts of light-houses were invented, such as those made of riveted sheet steel (like Esposende or Cabo Raso in Portugal) or of tubes with a large central pillar and lateral props. Other stonework towers were built too, but these were on land, far from the relentless onslaughts of the surf. Out at sea, the only viable method was the one invented for Eddystone III.

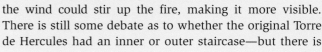

Relief keepers are airlifted onto the La Vieille lighthouse.

Millions of waves (at a rate of one every five seconds) had dashed against the rock on which John Smeaton had created the first modern lighthouse, when three new techniques revolutionized lighthouses, both on land and at sea. The first was their method of construction. In the late 1950s, lighthouses started to be designed in three main pieces, and the structure resembled a huge telescopic shaft topped with a cup-and-ball type design. The three pieces were built on dry land. The first was the base, which was to lie on the seabed; it was concave, made of pre-stressed concrete and had a cylindrical hole drilled through it. The second piece was a cylinder, designed to slide into the hole in the base. The third was a platform (the cup-and-ball), often made of metal, which housed the lantern room, the helipad and the shelter. The hollow, floating base, plugged with the equally hollow cylinder, was towed horizontally out to the site of the future lighthouse. Once the flood-gates were opened, the base and its cylinder righted them-selves and then sank down and came to rest on an area of the seabed that had been levelled beforehand. The water inside the base was then replaced with sand. At this stage, the top of the cylinder projected only slightly above water level. When the sea was calm, the platform was towed out on pontoons, the water was pumped out of the cylinder, and the platform was fitted into the top (like the ball in the cup). The piston floated, rising up as it slid into the base; when the platform reached its predetermined height, cement was injected between the base and the bottom of the cylinder so that the latter could not sink

down any further. Finally, the structure was electrified—and a new lighthouse was ready to shine.

The second revolution was the helicopter. Before it came into widespread use, lighthouse keepers had seemed like voluntary prisoners, and relieving crews was fraught with danger. Sometimes, a cable had had to be attached to the top of the tower, with the other end tied to a boat waiting well out beyond the reefs; a two-way system hoisted provisions up and brought keepers down over the raging sea. More often, the keepers were left stranded on their rock for weeks, until the sea became calm again. In 1946, a BBC journalist landed on Bishop Rock to broadcast Christmas greetings; he was unable to leave for four weeks, when he was finally rescued by cable. His plight had touched the whole country—but this was the daily lot of the light-house keeper. The advent of the helicopter made this a thing of the past. A helicopter could fly over the highest waves, and it could hover while the keeper was hoisted up, even if the manoeuvre was still dangerous. In 1973, Trinity House built a landing platform on top of the Wolf Rock lighthouse. The other British off-shore lighthouses soon had heli-pads of their own. Lighthouses no longer looked like pawns in a chess game; they had become queens.

The third revolution was automation. Thanks to the helicopter, the equipment could be maintained regardless of weather conditions. Candles no longer needed to be snuffed every half-hour, and the lights no longer needed keepers. Lighting techniques had come a long way since Sostratus of Cnidos and the lighthouse of Alexandria.

The original function of a lighthouse is to shine, and the earliest lights were simple fires, visible from several kilometres away. The two earliest such lights in Europe probably shone from a tower in Boulogne and from its counterpart in Dover (whose ruins still exist), sometime around AD 53. But lighting methods had not changed two hundred years later, when the Torre de Hercules was built at La Coruña in Spain. In fact, lighthouses did not evolve much at all until the end of the seven-teenth century. Before this time, a fire was lit, which burned more or less brightly according to its size and to the wind. Wood was consu-med at an alarming rate, and the logs had to be transported to the tower—lighthouses are rarely situated on the edge of a forest—then hoisted to the top. The braziers were made of wrought iron and shaped like an openwork bowl so that the wind could stir up the fire, making it more visible. There is still some debate as to whether the original Torre de Hercules had an inner or outer staircase—but there is

Kish, one of the first prefabricated lighthouses.

The use of helicopters transformed lighthouses: the Needles, before and after, with its helipad.

no doubt that it had a great many steps, and that keepers had to carry up large bundles of firewood. It was clear that a more concentrated form of fuel would be easier to transport—and in England, from the sixteenth century onwards, coal was used to feed the fires. Just one of these primitive lighthouses could consume two hundred tons of coal a year and up to three or four tons on a single stormy night. Those cartloads of coal had to be hauled over great distances, in the days before roads. An isolated rock lighthouse obviously could not be supplied this way, so Eddystone was lit at first with tallow candles, which had the advantage of being more compact, even if they were not as bright. Even though Eddystone II had been destroyed by fire in 1755, no better solution had been found when Smeaton was designing Eddystone III, so a 24-candle candelabrum was installed in the lantern at the top. Candles required constant attention; but in exchange, the keepers salvaged the leftover tallow and used it as barter.

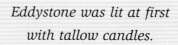

One of the candles used on Eddystone.

Towards the end of the eighteenth century, oil lamps finally replaced candles. Different oils were used in different countries: olive oil was used in lamps in the south, while whale oil was used in the north. In South Africa, lighthouse lanterns even used oil from the lubricating gland under a sheep's tail. A light could use up 3,315 litres (875 gallons) a year of this "Cape oil", and given the fact that one sheep's tail produces a teaspoon of oil, imagine the number of sheep's tails needed to supply a lighthouse for a year.

Visibility remained a problem. Around 1780, several inventors reached the same conclusion: instead of having a light that shone upwards and downwards, a parabolic mirror could focus the beam in one spot. Teulère, who built the tower that still stands at Cordouan, attempted this. Thomas Smith and Robert Stevenson were among the first to develop a complex system which became standard for several years: an oil lamp was inserted into a slit at the back of a parabolic mirror and placed so that its multiple wicks were right in the middle of the reflector. Many lighthouses were thus equipped with a battery of reflectors—three or four superposed rings of six, seven or eight reflectors.

Three further inventions (two French and one Swiss) gave the lights greater luminosity. Aimé Argand, a scientist from Geneva, had the idea of using a circular wick, which would burn at both ends, and would burn even better when protected by the invention of Quinquet, a Frenchman who had invented "lamp glass"—actually a transparent chimney. The Frenchman Carcel then invented a pump that injected

One of the first reflectors.

pressurised fuel into the wick. Apart from the use of new fuels, there were no new developments until the late nineteenth century. The French, who were at the forefront of lighting techniques, perfected rapeseed oil, which was refined after being treated with sulphuric acid. Before long it was widely used, being cheaper and of more regular quality than other kinds of fuel. However, this hegemony (which suited Normandy, where rapeseed was produced) lasted only thirty years, when kerosene became the chief fuel, until acetylene lamps arrived. Acetylene gas, produced from calcium carbide and water, was discovered by the Englishman Willson in 1892. Four years later, the Frenchmen Hess and Claude (the latter also invented the neon tube) discovered a way of compressing and storing acetylene, which generated five to ten times as much light as other fuels. In one century, lighting techniques had progressed from risky bonfires to powerful and regular beams. And finally, the French physicist Jean Fresnel (1788-1827) invented his revolutionary lens. Fresnel's role in the history of lighthouses is as important as that of the Englishman John Smeaton. The latter, with Eddystone III, had invented the technique for building towers on the open sea; the former made them visible. In the early nineteenth century, the most sophisticated form of lighting was a cylindrical assembly of twenty or so reflectors, each lit by an Argand lamp (with Quinquet's chimney and Carcel's pressurisation). Fuel consumption was considerable, and the system required constant maintenance. The ideal solution would be a single lamp, but it could not produce the strength of the multiple lighting system. Fresnel's answer was to focus the light with a circular magnifying glass, which would surround the flame—the problem being that the flame's rays spread above and below the glass. Fresnel decided to encircle the top and bottom of the flame with a series of prisms, which would reflect the rays horizontally, no matter where they came from. Fresnel tested his lens on the Cordouan lighthouse in 1823. The results was extraordinary. Ninety-seven per cent of the light from a naked flame shone outside the horizontal plane; with a reflector, the same flame still scattered eighty-three per cent of its light. Fresnel's lens, however, recuperated most of the rays that strayed upwards and downwards, and concentrated them on the horizontal plane, with a loss of only seventeen percent. In other words, efficiency was increased from three to eighty-three per cent and, thanks to the French physicist's invention, a flame was visible twenty-seven times farther away than before.

Eddystone was lit at first with tallow candles.

Admittedly, it was a complex device. Giant lenses weighing several tons were constructed, and they rotated on a mercury bath. At the foot of the tower of Créac'h—Europe's most powerful light—there is a lighthouse museum, which displays a series of these mastodons. With their glass scales they look like some kind of antediluvian trilobite, or prehistoric, transparent armadillo, yet they represented a triumph for science and technology. In the grand gallery of the first Universal Exhibition in 1851, a huge Fresnel lens was given pride of place, although Fresnel himself was not there to witness this: he had died in 1827, at the age of forty. His invention was further developed by his brother, Léonor, and in Scotland, by Alan Stevenson.

The lens that Fresnel tested on Cordouan in 1823.

The electrification of lighthouses would not change much, until halogen lighthouses were developed in the 1970s. From this point on, the old lenses were no longer necessary, as there was more than enough luminosity. Thanks to automation, a mechanism could change the lamps that had blown out. These lights were arranged in cylindrical batteries, much like the lanterns of the late eighteenth century.

But the end was near for the lighthouse. The beacons of today are invisible. They float, weightless, hundreds of kilometres above the sea and its reefs. The Global Positioning System is accurate to within a few metres. What use are these costly towers today, when GPS is less expensive than a good pair of binoculars? Sailors merely type in the geographical coordinates of the points to be circumnavigated and set their automatic pilot, which guides a ship from X to Y (even at night or in fog), negotiating points G, K, and Q and their reefs, with no need of a lighthouse. With modern techniques, a blind man can cross the Pacific single-handed. When ships are fewer and more automated, needing fewer ports of call, what good are lighthouses? Sooner or later, these shining sentries are doomed to obsolescence, as they keep watch over coasts that only interest pleasure craft and fishermen, who have no need of their warning lights.

Lighthouses were born in the age of steam. They had their heyday, but their usefulness expired with the advent of satellites and computers. Cordouan's sumptuous decoration is already deteriorating, even though this lighthouse was listed as a Historic Monument at the same time as Notre-Dame de Paris—and who still goes to see it? Does anyone still admire the 12,500 opaline slabs on the staircase of the Île Vierge lighthouse?

As a tribute to lighthouses, Philip and Guillaume Plisson have photographed all the lights along the Atlantic Rim. The monuments illustrated in this book are still working; they may have lost their keepers, but they still serve a purpose. Most are difficult to visit, because they are so inaccessible. This great photographer and his son spent 150 hours in a helicopter, countless days in a boat and a year of their lives documenting these future relics.

The solitude of the lighthouse keeper, on Kéréon.

(1) An earthquake destroyed what remained of the lighthouse of Alexandria in the fourteenth century AD.
(2) English prince who reigned over Aquitaine during a period when south-west France belonged to the British.
(3) Orders are defined by the focal distance of the lens: 1st order: 920 mm; 2nd order: 700 mm; 3rd order: 500 mm; 4th order: 250 mm; 5th order: 187.5 mm; 6th order: 150 mm.
(4) *Les feux de la mer*, Musée de la Marine, 7 October 1992 to 31 January 1993.

The Sein lighthouse.

Scotland

The Northern Lights

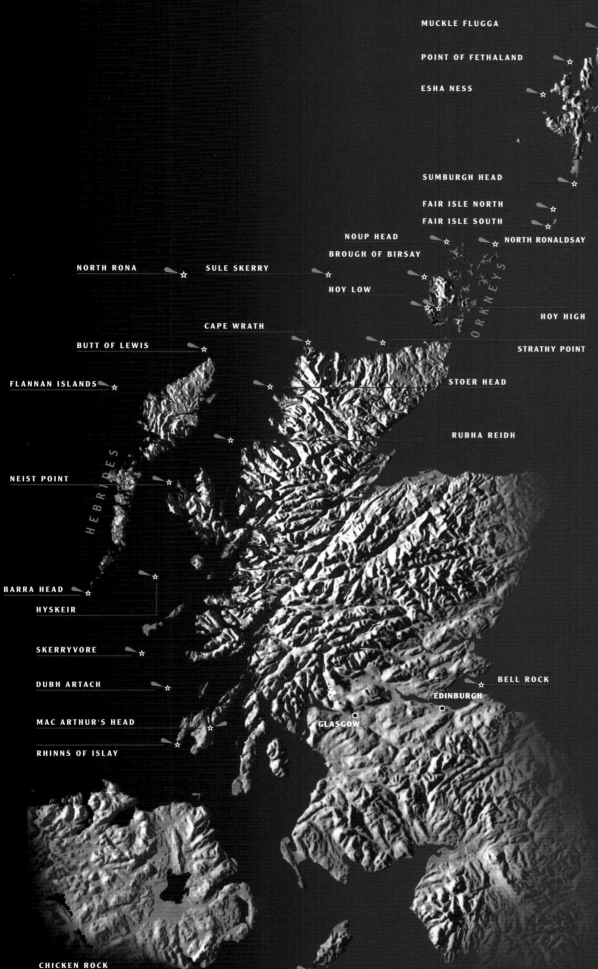

MUCKLE FLUGGA

POINT OF FETHALAND

ESHA NESS

SHETLAND

SUMBURGH HEAD

FAIR ISLE NORTH

FAIR ISLE SOUTH

NOUP HEAD

BROUGH OF BIRSAY

NORTH RONALDSAY

NORTH RONA

SULE SKERRY

HOY LOW

ORKNEYS

HOY HIGH

CAPE WRATH

BUTT OF LEWIS

STRATHY POINT

FLANNAN ISLANDS

STOER HEAD

RUBHA REIDH

HEBRIDES

NEIST POINT

BARRA HEAD

HYSKEIR

SKERRYVORE

DUBH ARTACH

BELL ROCK

EDINBURGH

MAC ARTHUR'S HEAD

GLASGOW

RHINNS OF ISLAY

Any landsman who decided to pin a flag on the map to mark every Scottish lighthouse would be in for a surprise: there are sixty along the Atlantic shoreline alone. Why so many? First of all, the area is particularly difficult to negotiate, with nine islands more than 5 kilometres (3 miles) long in the Shetlands, seventeen in the Orkneys and thirty-three in the Hebrides. And these islands are steep, edged with what look like basalt organ pipes, dotted with large quartz formations and have fearsome islets and reefs all around them, not to mention some of Europe's strongest tides. What business or trade could justify the extraordinary expense of constructing lighthouses in these wild and remote regions, where rocks outnumber even sheep?

Left

The inaccessible Barra Head lighthouse, 190 metres (623 feet) above the sea.

CHICKEN ROCK

The reasons become clear by looking at a globe. Despite Scotland's isolated position, it lies along the most direct route from Paris to New York. The British may call the south-west tip of England "Land's End", but Europe's most western headland is in Scotland: Ardnamurchan is 60 kilometres (40 miles) farther west than Land's End. This proximity to America made Scotland an important centre of maritime activity in the nineteenth century, the period when most lighthouses were built. At that time, a regular shipping route existed between Oban and the United States, although it's hard to imagine today, looking at this sleepy Scottish port. The early steamships were so uncomfortable that Charles Dickens could only describe his cabin in these terms: "a totally impractical, completely hopeless and profoundly absurd box", and passengers preferred to reduce the sea voyage as much as possible by taking the train as far as they could, which was to Oban.

The proximity to America made Scotland an important centre of maritime activity in the nineteenth century, the period when most lighthouses were built.

The Shetland Islands lie to the north of Scotland. They belong to Great Britain, yet they are nearer to Oslo, Stockholm or Copenhagen than to London. From the Shetlands, you could sail to Bergen, in Norway, in less time than it would take to sail to Edinburgh, the Scottish capital. All sea traffic coming from the Baltic or the White Sea and heading to America (or vice versa) passes by the Shetlands. When Great Britain was at war with Russia and Germany, this was the most important strategic route on the seas. Scotland was of prime naval importance. During the First World War, the major British naval base was Scapa Flow, in the Orkneys, between the Shetlands and Scotland. During the Cold War, the British nuclear submarines were based in Lossiemouth, north of Aberdeen. The construction of the Muckle Flugga lighthouse illustrates this strategic importance.

In 1853, Russia entered into a dispute with Turkey over the ownership of the provinces of Moldavia and Walachia. Great Britain and France backed the Turks. On 3 November 1853, Russia annihilated a Turkish squadron in the port of Sinop, and the Turkish allies declared war on the tsar. Task forces were sent out, followed by much bloodshed, but the main British tactic was the blockade. All Russian trade with the West could be stopped: the Turks controlled access to the Black Sea, England controlled the Channel from Dover and Scotland controlled the northern route, leading to the White Sea and the Baltic. The trouble was that the Scottish coasts were hardly beaconed at all; how could a fleet intercept the Russian navy on its way from Archangel or Murmansk, if it was "intercepted" on its way by the Scottish rocks? In a single memorable night in 1811, the Navy lost three ships and two thousand men there—more than the British losses during the Battle of Trafalgar six years before. Lighthouses were needed desperately, by the following year, if possible.

A ship passing Ardnamurchan.

A temporary light was therefore built in twenty-six days at the top of an inaccessible islet, 60 metres (197 feet) high. Four years later, in 1858, a permanent lighthouse had been erected there and a new star began to shine: this was the Muckle Flugga lighthouse, the most northern on the Atlantic Rim. The Crimean War had ended twenty months earlier with a Russian defeat. The blockade had not been efficient, and today few people even know what the fighting was about, but at the far north of the British Isles, the darkness of the night is still pierced by two white flashes every twenty seconds.

Muckle Flugga was designed and built by the brothers David and Thomas Stevenson. The latter's son, Robert Louis, was only eight at the time; it would be another twenty years before he published *Travels with a Donkey in the Cévennes*, and he did not make his name until *Treasure Island* in 1883. But Robert Louis Stevenson—the globetrotter who died in Samoa, the successful author and founding father of the adventure story—was actually the black sheep of his family. The Stevensons did not write books: they built lighthouses. These Scottish engineers included his grandfather Robert, his uncles Alan and David, his father Thomas and his nephews David A. and Charles. Scotland's most famous lighthouses—Bell Rock, Skerryvore, Muckle Flugga, Chicken Rock, Bound Skerry, Dubh Artach and so on—were all designed by one of the Stevensons; from 1854 to 1880, the novelist's father and uncle built twenty-eight lighthouses—more than one a year. This dynasty reigned for more than a century over the design of Scottish lighthouses and built practically all the substructures that still exist today.

In 1786, an Act of Parliament granted Scotland its own lighthouse and pilot authority. The "Commissioners of Northern Lights' immediately set out to find a chief engineer, finally appointing thirty-four-year-old Thomas Smith, the son of a master mariner to the position. He knew nothing of architecture or engineering, but was an expert in lamp-making. He had designed Edinburgh's system of street lighting and perfected a reflector consisting of a mosaic of mirrors, which concentrated the light better than its continental rivals had. Smith went to England to perfect his knowledge of lighthouses and learn what he needed to know about construction techniques. Torn between his lighting business and the long hours spent surveying the wild Scottish coast, Thomas Smith soon found he needed an assistant—and met the man he needed at church. Robert Stevenson was the son of a Glasgow widow; his mother had taken him to Edinburgh to do his studies. Mrs Stevenson and her son met Thomas Smith as they belonged to the same congregation. Smith made nineteen-year-old Robert his apprentice in 1791, and in 1792, the widowed Mrs Stevenson married Thomas Smith. In 1799, Robert Stevenson married Jane, Thomas Smith's eldest daughter from his first marriage.

Skerryvore, isolated on its reef.
Landing on it was the first problem.

Meanwhile, Robert Stevenson was installing reflectors in the Port Patrick and Cumbrae lighthouses and had returned to Glasgow to study civil engineering. He had followed the construction of the two lights of the Pentland Skerries. When the building was finished, ill-tempered winds made him decide to return by road rather than by sea; the rest of his team, all travelling by boat, were drowned. Between two building projects, he studied chemistry and mathematics; and above all, in 1797, he succeeded his stepfather as chief engineer of the Northern Lights. The apprentice had become the master. His first independent construction was the Inchkeith lighthouse, on the east coast, but he was already absorbed in the problems of building Bell Rock.

Bell Rock was the most dangerous reef on the east coast (56°26'N, 2°23'W), in the North Sea (far to the other side of the Atlantic Rim, the subject of this book, but nonetheless important to Scottish lighthouse history). Attempts had been made to place beacons on this great reef since the fourteenth century, but how could anything be built on a mass of stone that disappeared under 4 metres (13 feet) of water at high tide? Compared to Bell Rock, Eddystone was child's play. A lighthouse had never yet been built on a submerged reef.[1] In the early days of work on the rock, Stevenson found himself stranded with thirty-two men when the boat broke its moorings, leaving them no way to get off the rock. The tide was rising, and they would have all drowned if a supply boat, on its way to deliver mail, had not rescued them. The team stayed at sea the whole time—it took from four to six hours to get back to land—living first on an accompanying boat, then in a three-storey barrack on pilings, built during the summer of 1807. Work continued on the mainland during the winter: Stevenson had decided to build Bell Rock according to the method perfected by Smeaton on Eddystone III: the whole edifice was prefabricated in interlocking granite blocks, each of which weighed up to several tons. They were cut and shaped by hand, loaded onto a sailing ship, unloaded perilously onto the reef, then pushed by hand (a railway had been laid) to the site of the lighthouse and finally hoisted up by hand. When the Bell Rock lighthouse was inaugurated in 1811, it weighed 2,076 tons.

Robert Stevenson continued to build lighthouses, notably a tower on the Isle of May (1816, on the east coast), a double light facing Chicken Rock on the Isle of Man (1818) and another clinging to the breathtaking ridge of Barra Head (1833). This made sixteen lighthouses in all, not to mention Skerryvore, which he had dreamed of and helped to design, and which his son Alan finally built.

For ships sailing from America to Oban, but also to Glasgow and Liverpool, the friendly light of Barra Head signalled from the top of its 190-metre (620-feet) cliff. Yet the welcome could be deceptive, as ships were sometimes flung onto the rocks of Sgeir Mhor (pronounced *scare vore*, Gaelic for "big rock")

"It will be a most desolate position for a lighthouse—the Bell Rock and Eddystone a joke to it."

Chicken Rock was destroyed by fire in 1960. Its keepers were rescued in extremis.

thirty miles farther on. From 1790 until the new lighthouse was inaugurated in 1844, thirty ships were wrecked on these eight miles of reef south of Tiree, which seemed to be the only way of landing there. In 1814, however, two distinguished visitors landed and lived to tell the tale: the engineer Robert Stevenson, crowned with glory for his triumph on Bell Rock, and the writer Walter Scott, famous for the success of *The Lady of the Lake*. Scott later described this portion of the trip: "We pull through a very heavy swell with great difficulty, and approach a tremendous surf dashing over black pointed rocks. Our rowers, however, get the boat into a quiet creek between two rocks, where we contrive to land well wetted…The rock was carefully measured by Mr. S. It will be a most desolate position for a lighthouse—the Bell Rock and Eddystone a joke to it …" And indeed, it was another thirty years before a light shone from Skerryvore.

Robert Stevenson was sixty-six when construction began in 1837; this was no age for leaping about on rocks, and building Skerryvore was a serious challenge—the water churning over this inaccessible reef in calm weather provides ample demonstration. Moreover, the engineer was too engrossed in other projects (bridges and ports) to undertake single-handedly the construction of the highest pre-Victorian lighthouse. So he entrusted the task to his eldest son, Alan, who had already made a name for himself by developing and perfecting the Fresnel lens.

When Alan Stevenson undertook this giant lighthouse, he benefited from an unprecedented series of developments: the Eddystone "building block" technique, the idea of temporary barracks on the reef (perfected by his father

Neist Point, on the west coast of the Isle of Skye.
The keepers' lodgings have been turned into guesthouses.

on Bell Rock), explosives and the steam engine (pioneered by his homonym, George Stephenson). The tower should have been easy to build, but it turned into a nightmare that ruined the health of its designer. Work began in 1837 with the opening of a granite quarry on the Isle of Mull and the construction of a special steamship to transport the rocks out to the reef.

The year 1838 was spent hollowing out foundations with explosives then building a temporary tower to house the workmen— who toiled sixteen hours a day. Initially, some of them slept in crevices in the rock and were soaked to the skin twenty-four hours a day, but the barracks was finally ready at the end of the season. In November, a particularly violent storm swept it away, destroying the

Maintenance workers reach Dubh Artach by helicopter.

result of an entire year's work. In 1839, work began again with a vengeance. A new barracks was built; this was a tower on metal piles, 18 metres (60 feet) high (as tall as a six-storey building), each piece of which had to be shipped out to the reef and carried up the slippery rocks. The foundation pit for the lighthouse was excavated: it was a circle 12.80 metres (42 feet) in diameter, blasted out of the granite with 296 charges of explosive. It took twenty men 217 days to extract 2,000 tons from a rock that was four times harder than the granite of which the tower would be built. Work had begun in 1837, the workmen had landed on Skerryvore in 1838 and finally, on 4 July 1840, the first stone was laid. The granite for the tower was sent, roughly hewn, to the island of Tiree, where the blocks were shaped. The easiest stones required 85 hours of labour, and the most complex up to 320 hours each. Some 4,300 stones had to be cut, then transported by sea and landed on the rock in unimaginably difficult conditions. In 1840, a storm prevented the steamship from approaching for two full weeks; the workmen were left stranded in their shaky, cramped shelter. At the end of the 1840 season, after three years of work, a stump 2.49 metres (8 feet) high had been built on Skerryvore—but the worst was over. A year later, the tower was 18 metres (59 feet) tall, but wintry storms could still hurl rocks onto the top of it.

In 1843, Alan Stevenson became chief engineer to the Northern Lights, and his brother Thomas took over the task of completing Skerryvore. The tallest lighthouse of its time, it stood 42 metres (138 feet) and was inaugurated on 1 February 1844. It had cost £86,977, 17s and 7d —the price of a large warship.

The unique architectural feature of Skerryvore was its weight. Gravity anchored the tower to the rock, and its solid base served as ballast. Although this granite pillar measured 12.80 metres (42 feet) at its base, the ten superposed chambers were only 3.60 metres (12 feet) in diameter. This was a fairly uncomfortable arrangement, especially when the keepers were stormbound for thirteen weeks at a time, as they were in 1865. Instead of an interior staircase (as is in French lighthouses) there were ladders,

which facilitated rapid evacuation. Their usefulness was demonstrated in 1954 when Skerryvore was ravaged by fire (the repairs took five years).

Alan Stevenson resigned from his post, exhausted by the construction of his masterpiece and disabled by permanent lumbago. His younger brother David became the new engineer of the Northern Lights, a position he was soon to share with his other brother Thomas (who had finished Skerryvore). In 1851, at the tip of a headland in the Orkneys, they built Hoy High, which looks like a sort of barracks overhung by a 17-metre (56-foot) candle. In 1861, they built the light of McArthur's Head; it looks like a sort of country cemetery with white-painted walls, which in daylight are almost more visible than the lighthouse itself. In 1862, at the Butt of Lewis, they built a mock village school, except that there is no village and a stonework tower dwarfs the playground. Many other, simpler lighthouses were also built, but the Stevenson bothers still had to face two challenges, in the form of two rock lighthouses: Dubh Artach and Chicken Rock.

The first was near Skerryvore, not far from the island of Iona (whose cemetery contains the tombs of forty-two Celtic kings, including that of a certain Macbeth), and the basalt island of Staffa, site of Fingal's cave (set to music by Mendelssohn). The fearsome reef of Dubh Artach had celebrated the end of 1865 in its own macabre fashion, by wrecking twenty-four ships on the night of 30 December alone. The major problem here was landing on the reef: in 1869, the workmen could only land on the rock every four days. Fortunately, the reef was big enough to accommodate a temporary barracks, like those on Bell Rock

and Skerryvore; this particular shelter was 23.46 metres (77 feet) above sea level, but waves still swept over it. The Dubh Artach light was inaugurated on 1 November 1872. By this time, the Stevenson brothers were already busy working on the last seemingly impossible lighthouse of the Northern Lights: Chicken Rock. Situated off the coast of the Isle of Man in the Irish Sea, this reef was only visible at low tide. In 1818, the eldest Stevenson had already built two lighthouses not far from there, but they were often invisible due to fog. The reef would finally be beaconed by his grandsons. Chicken Rock was inaugurated early in 1875, but was destroyed by fire eighty-five years later; this time, the keepers were only saved *in extremis*.

The lighthouse keepers on the Flannan Islands, however, met a more mysterious fate: they simply disappeared. The Flannan Islands lie far to the north-west of the Hebrides; they are also called the "Seven Hunters', although there are more than seven of them. The largest is Eilean Mor, which is where David Stevenson's sons, David A. and Charles, built a lighthouse in 1895-1899. They chose the most visible spot, at the top of a cliff 87 metres (285 feet) high. Two staircases were carved out of the rock, one on each face of Eilean Mor, so that boats could land on either side, depending on the direction the wind was blowing. Above the west landing stage was a stonework platform, equipped with a crane, to unload the blocks onto a little funicular railway, which had also been carved out of the rock. The lighthouse is a massive tower, 23 metres (75 feet) high, with a keepers' house adjoining it.

During the night of 15 December 1900, the steamship *Archer,* coming from Philadelphia on its way to Edinburgh, sailed past the Flannan Islands without seeing a light from the lighthouse, although the silhouette of the tower was visible on top of Eilean Mor. Why wasn't it lit? When the captain reached his destination, he made a report to the Commissioners of Northern Lights, who warned the *Hesperus,* the ship that was to relieve the keepers. The crew of the *Hesperus* dropped anchor near the island's

The shelter was 23.46 metres (77 feet) above sea level, but waves still passed over it.

east coast, but saw no sign of life. They managed to land one of the relief keepers, who climbed the two hundred odd steps up to the lighthouse. The doors were closed, the fire was out, the clock had stopped and the beds were unmade. The story goes that there was a cold meal on the table. One of the keepers' oilskins was hanging on its peg, but the other two were missing. The three men had vanished.

There had been a terrible storm, which had ripped the grass off the cliff-top over a distance of 10 metres (33 feet). Near the crane, at a height of 35 metres (115 feet), a box of equipment had been pulverised. The keepers had noted all this in their logbook and had then disappeared, on 15 December in the afternoon. The most far-fetched explanations were suggested, but one hundred years after the disappearance of the three keepers of Eilean Mor, the mystery of the empty lighthouse remains unsolved.

There are no keepers on the Flannan Islands today: the lighthouse was automated in 1971, and the huge Fresnel lens was replaced by a more modern one. However, its light still worked on acetylene, whereas 200 miles farther south, the lighthouse of Rathlin O'Birne was designed to operate on nuclear energy—but this is no longer in Scotland, but in Ireland.

(1) The fort of Bugio, in Portugal (see the chapter «The Iberian Lighthouses») had been constructed in the same conditions, but it was not yet a lighthouse.

The Flannan Islands, whose keepers mysteriously vanished in 1900.

Muckle Flugga

The entire Atlantic coast,
with its 210 lighthouses, stretches
south from Muckle Flugga (towards
the top of the page). This is, quite
literally, the end of the world: it
took one year to find the helicopter
to take the photograph above,
and a four-hour hike at night for the
photograph to the right.

Region - Shetland
Position - 60°51'3"N - 0°53'0"W
Year of construction - 1854
Engineers - Thomas and David Stevenson
Height - 20 metres/66 feet
Height above sea level - 66 metres/216 feet
Date of automation - 1995
Visibility - 25 miles
Optics - Fresnel
Lights - 2 white flashes. 20 seconds
Helipad - Yes
Open to the public - No
Inhabited - No

Fair Isle North

The small lighthouse on the northern point of Fair Isle is set slightly back from the coast; an enormous foghorn stands at the edge of a cliff. To reach it, a small bridge was built between the islands, with railings from one end to the other, so that the lighthouse keepers would not be blown off the edge.

Region - Shetland Islands
Position - 59°33'2"N - 1°36'5"W
Year of construction - 1892
Engineer - David A. Stevenson
Height - 14 metres/46 feet
Height above sea level - 80 metres/262 feet
Date of automation - 1981
Visibility - 22 miles
Optics - Revolving light with reflectors
Lights - 2 flashing lights. 30 seconds
Foghorn - 3 signals, 1.5 seconds long.
45 seconds
Helipad - Yes
Open to the public - No
Inhabited - No

Fair Isle South

Fair Isle South was the last Scottish lighthouse to have a keeper. When it was automated on 31 March 1998, lighthouse keepers lowered the Northern Lights flag for the last time, folded it and presented it to Princess Anne (below, with handbag). She immediately offered it to the oldest lighthouse keeper, Angus Hutchison. The entire staff of the Northern Lights gathered for this poignant ceremony on this remote island. It was the end of an era.

Region - Shetland Islands
Position - 59°30'9"N - 1°39'0"W
Year of construction - 1892
Engineer - David A. Stevenson
Height - 26 metres/85 feet
Height above sea level - 32 metres/105 feet
Date of automation - 31 March 1998

Visibility - 24 miles
Optics - Fresnel
Lights - 4 white flashes. 30 seconds
Foghorn - 2 signals. 60 seconds
Helipad - Yes
Open to the public - No
Inhabited - No

North Ronaldsay

With the wind against the current, the sea churns in front of North Ronaldsay. The last keeper stands at the top of the lighthouse, while the equipment for automating it has been parked at the base. In the foreground, a medieval tower, which was used as a landmark on this island battered by storms.

Region - Orkney Islands
Position - 59°23'4"N - 2°22'8"W
Year of construction - 1854
Engineer - Thomas Smith
Height - 42 metres/138 feet
Height above sea level - 41 metres/135 feet
Date of automation - 1998
Visibility - 19 miles
Optics - Fresnel
Lights - 1 flash. 10 seconds
Foghorn - 5 signals. 60 seconds
Helipad - No
Open to the public - No
Inhabited - No

Sule Skerry

Like Ronaldsay, Sule Skerry is a flat island which would be hard to see if it did not have a lighthouse. The squat tower was constructed by David Stevenson, from the third generation in this incredible family of lighthouse-builders.

The keeper Ronnie Cooper spent seventeen years on this tiny, treeless island—which has the highest concentration of nesting puffins in Scotland.

Region - Orkney Islands
Position - 59°5'0"N - 4°24'3"W
Year of construction - 1895
Engineer - David A. Stevenson
Height - 27 metres/88 feet
Height above sea level - 34 metres/111 feet
Date of automation - 1982
Visibility - 19 miles
Optics - Fresnel
Lights - 2 white flashes. 15 seconds
Helipad - Yes
Open to the public - No
Inhabited - No

Hoy Low

The Orkneys are one of the most beautiful places on the Atlantic coast. The Hoy Low lighthouse stands at the base of a 1,150-feet cliff. Once past this lighthouse, you reach Stromness, where each house, built right alongside the next one, has its own quay. Stewart Taylor is in charge of upkeep for all the lighthouses on the Orkney Islands—it takes him one month to see them all.

Region - Orkney Islands
Position - 58°56'5"N - 3°18'4"W
Year of construction - 1851
Engineer - Alan Stevenson
Height - 12 metres/39 feet
Height above sea level - 17 metres/56 feet
Date of automation - 1966
Visibility - 15 miles
Optics - Fresnel
Lights - 1 white flash. 3 seconds
Helipad - No
Open to the public - No
Inhabited - No

Hoy High

Hoy High stands opposite Stromness. Behind it stretches the immense Scapa Flow Bay, from which the Royal Navy sailed for the Battle of Jutland during World War I. Today, supertankers loaded with North Sea oil are based here. In the foreground, a golf course (a sport invented by the Scots), where the islands' fishermen, boat crews, businessmen and farmers meet on weekends.

Region - Orckney Islands
Position - 58°56'5"N - 3'18'4"W
Year of construction - 1851
Engineer - Alan Stevenson
Height - 33 metres/108 feet
Height above sea level - 35 metres/
115 feet
Date of automation - 1978
Visibility - 20 miles
Optics - Fresnel
Lights - 1 white flash. 8 seconds
Helipad - No
Open to the public - No
Inhabited - Yes

Cape Wrath

The northwest tip of mainland Scotland ends at Cape Wrath. All the petroleum products from the refineries located on the Shetland and Orkney islands pass by this point heading west. These photographs were taken shortly before the lighthouse was automated, but progress had already made inroads here—as illustrated by the small bulb in Alex Smith's hand, which is far more powerful than the enormous lamps of the past.

Region - Northwest
Position - 58°37'5"N - 4°59'87"W
Year of construction - 1828
Engineer - Robert Stevenson
Height - 20 metres/66 feet
Height above sea level - 122 metres/ 400 feet
Date of automation - 1998
Visibility - 24 miles
Optics - Revolving light with reflectors
Lights - 4 white flashes. 30 seconds
Foghorn - 1 signal, 6 seconds long. 90 seconds
Helipad - Yes
Open to the public - No

Region - West
Position - 58°31'0"N - 6°15'7"W
Year of construction - 1862
Engineer - David A. Stevenson
Height - 37 metres/121 feet
Height above sea level - 52 metres/171 feet
Date of automation - 1998
Visibility - 25 miles
Optics - Revolving light with reflectors
Lights - 1 flash. 5 seconds
Foghorn - 2 signals. 30 seconds
Helipad - No
Open to the public - No

Butt of Lewis

Lewis Island, the northernmost of the Outer Hebrides, is so windy that trees don't even grow here. The peat soil gives way with each step. This would be a no-man's land if it weren't for the emerald-colored grass—which only grows in one season. The rest of the time, the vegetation is burned brown by salt blown up with the sea mist. The keeper Donald Micheal put on his uniform one last time for this photograph: several weeks later, he left his post, replaced by automation.

Barra Head

The Barra Head lighthouse stands at the top of a sheer rocky spur (see also photograph on page 16). Constructing the lighthouse itself was not a problem—it is only 18 metres (59 feet) high—but unloading the material and equipment, and hauling it by hand 190 metres (625 feet) above sea level was an extraordinary feat. As for the three families of the lighthouse keepers, they had to withstand both solitude and a lack a privacy.

Region - Far west
Position - 56°47'1"N - 7°39'2"W
Year of construction - 1833
Engineer - Robert Stevenson
Height - 18 metres/59 feet
Height above sea level -190 metres/625 feet
Date of automation - 1980
Visibility - 21 miles
Optics - Revolving light with reflectors
Lights - 1 white flash. 3 seconds
Helipad - No
Open to the public - No
Inhabited - No

Region - Southwest
Position - 56°19'4"N - 7°6'9"W
Year of construction - 1844
Engineer - Alan Stevenson
Height - 48 metres/157 feet
Height above sea level -
46 metres/151 feet
Date of automation - 1994
Visibility - 26 miles
Optics - Fresnel
Lights - 1 white flash. 10 seconds
Foghorn - 1 signal. 60 seconds
Helipad - Yes
Visistable - No
Inhabited - No

Skerryvore was the first large
lighthouse to be built on a reef off the
western Scottish coast. Inaugurated
in 1844, it is still the highest lighthouse
in Great Britain. The interior is a narrow
vertical passageway in which keepers
climbed from one chamber to another
using ladders. During storms, the wind
blew so hard that the keepers couldn't
hear themselves speak.

Skerryvore

Region - Southwest
Position - 55°40'4"N - 6°30'8"W
Year of construction - 1825
Engineer - Robert Stevenson
Height - 29 metres/95 feet
Height above sea level - 46 metres/151 feet
Date of automation - 1998
Visibility - 24 miles
Optics - Revolving light with reflectors
Lights - 1 white flash, 5 seconds
Foghorn - 3 signals, 90 seconds
Helipad - No
Open to the public - No
Inhabited - No

Rhinns of Islay

The coast of Islay is dotted with distilleries, while the bagpipes are Irish. The residents here feel more Irish than Scottish, which makes sense in that the lighthouse is visible from Ireland. On 19 February 1998, the helicopter (right) picked up the keepers Duncan Leslie and Jim Bain for the last time; from this date on, the lighthouse has been automated.

Point of Fethaland

Region - Shetland	Optics - Revolving light with reflectors
Position - 60°38'1"N - 1°18'6"W	Lights - 3 flashes. 15 seconds
Year of construction - 1977	Helipad - No
Engineer - P. H. Hyslop	Open to the public - No
Height - 7 metres/23 feet	Inhabited - No
Visibility - 24 miles white, 20 miles red	

Here are nine Scottish lighthouses constructed between 1854 and 1977, some on precipitous slopes, others at water's edge. All of them (with the exception of the last three, Point of Fethaland, Strathy Point and North Rona) were built by one of three generations of Stevensons, from Robert to David A. 125 years later. For more than 100 years, this family built most of the lighthouses in Scotland. The "black sheep," Thomas's son Robert Louis Stevenson, refused to follow the family tradition and became famous for his books, including, among others, *Treasure Island.*

Esha Ness

Region - Shetland	Date of automation - 1974
Position - 60°29'3"N - 1°37'6"W	Visibility - 25 miles
Year of construction - 1929	Optics - Revolving light with reflectors
Engineer - David A. Stevenson	Lights - 1 white flash. 12 seconds
Height - 12 metres/39 feet	Helipad - No
Height above sea level -	Open to the public - No
66 metres/216 feet	Inhabited - No

Sumburgh Head

Region - Shetland Islands	Date of automation - 1991
Position - 60°51'3"N - 0°53'0"W	Visibility - 23 miles
Year of construction - 1854	Optics - Fresnel
Engineers - Thomas & David	Lights - 3 white flashes. 20 seconds
Stevenson	Foghorn - 1 signal. 30 seconds
Height - 17 metres/56 feet	Helipad - No
Height above sea level -	Open to the public - No
91 metres/299 feet	Inhabited - Yes

Noup Head

Region - Orkney Islands	Date of automation - 1964
Position - 59°19'9"N - 3°04'0"W	Visibility - 22 miles
Year of construction - 1898	Optics - Fresnel
Engineer - David A. Stevenson	Lights - 1 flash. 30 seconds
Height - 24 metres/79 feet	Helipad - No
Height above sea level -	Open to the public - No

Strathy Point

Region - North
Position - 58°36'0"N - 4°01'0"W
Year of construction - 1958
Engineer - P. H. Hyslop
Height - 14 metres/46 feet
Height above sea level -
35 metres/115 feet
Date of automation - 1997

Visibility - 27 miles
Optics - Fresnel
Lights - 1 white flash. 20 seconds
Foghorn - 4 signals. 90 seconds
Helipad - No
Open to the public - No
Inhabited - No

North Rona

Region - Far northwest
Position - 59°07'3"N - 5°48'8"W
Year of construction - 1984
Engineer - R.J. Mackay
Height - 9 metres/30 feet
Height above sea level -
114 metres/374 feet

Visibility - 24 miles
Optics - Fresnel
Lights - 3 white flashes. 20 seconds
Helipad - Yes
Open to the public - No
Inhabited - No

Flannan Islands

Region - West. 15 miles NW of Lewis
Position - 58°17'3"N - 7°35'4"W
Year of construction - 1899
Engineer - David A. Stevenson
Height - 23 metres/75 feet
Height above sea level -
101 metres/331 feet

Date of automation - 1971
Visibility - 20 miles
Optics - Fresnel
Lights - 2 white flashes. 30 seconds
Helipad - Yes
Open to the public - No
Inhabited - No

Hyskeir

Region - West
Position - 56°47'1"N - 7°39'2"W
Year of construction - 1904
Engineer - David A. Stevenson
Height - 39 metres/128 feet
Height above sea level -
42 metres/138 feet

Date of automation - 1997
Visibility - 24 miles
Optics - Fresnel
Lights - 3 white flashes. 30 seconds
Helipad - Yes
Open to the public - No
Inhabited - No

Dubh Artach

Region - West
Position - 56°8'00"N - 6°37'9"W
Year of construction - 1872
Engineers - Thomas & David
Stevenson
Height - 38 metres/125 feet
Height above sea level -
44 metres/144 feet

Date of automation - 1971
Visibility - 20 miles
Optics - Fresnel
Lights - 2 white flashes. 30 seconds
Foghorn - 2 signals. 45 seconds
Helipad - Yes
Open to the public - No
Inhabited - No

Ireland

Celtic Magic

The Flannan Islands, whose lighthouse keepers vanished so mysteriously, are named after an Irish hermit. Iona Abbey, also in Scotland, not far from the Dubh Artach lighthouse, was founded by an Irish warlord, who sought forgiveness for the bloodshed he had caused in his homeland. South of Skerryvore, in the distilleries that dot the coasts of the Scottish island of Islay, there is little doubt that the former name for whisky, *usquebaugh,* is of Irish origin. Farther to the south-east, still in Scotland, the lighthouse built in 1788 by Thomas Smith at the top of the Mull of Kintyre illuminates a large island nearby, less than ten miles to the west: Green Erin, in Ireland. When the first lights shone out over the Atlantic Rim, Scotland was still an extension of Ireland, and there was some confusion about where one ended and the other began.

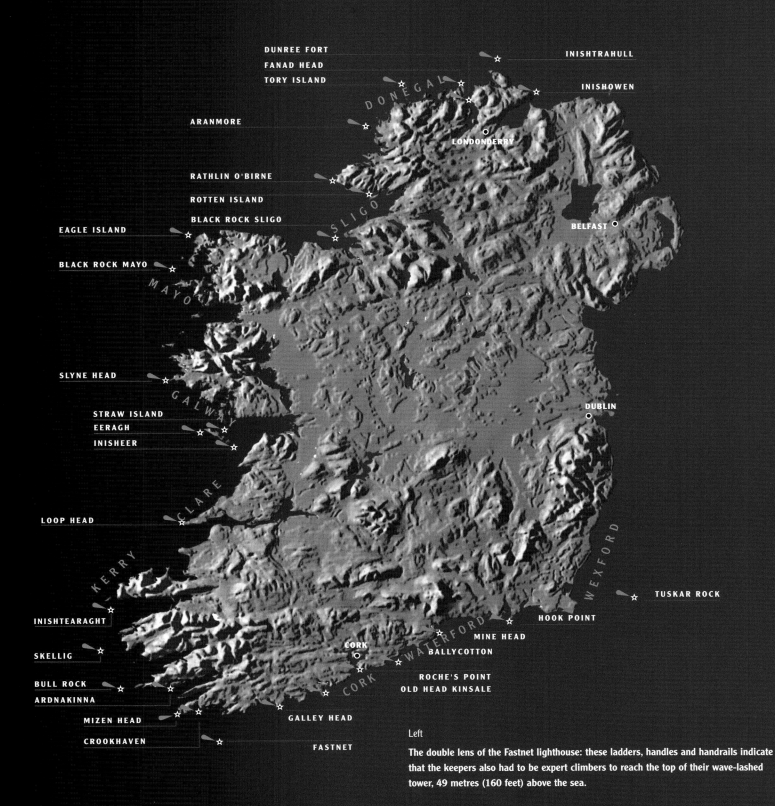

DUNREE FORT
FANAD HEAD
TORY ISLAND
INISHTRAHULL
INISHOWEN
ARANMORE
LONDONDERRY
RATHLIN O'BIRNE
ROTTEN ISLAND
BLACK ROCK SLIGO
BELFAST
EAGLE ISLAND
BLACK ROCK MAYO
SLYNE HEAD
STRAW ISLAND
EERAGH
INISHEER
DUBLIN
LOOP HEAD
TUSKAR ROCK
HOOK POINT
MINE HEAD
INISHTEARAGHT
CORK
BALLYCOTTON
SKELLIG
ROCHE'S POINT
OLD HEAD KINSALE
BULL ROCK
ARDNAKINNA
MIZEN HEAD
GALLEY HEAD
CROOKHAVEN
FASTNET

DONEGAL
SLIGO
MAYO
GALWAY
CLARE
KERRY
WEXFORD
WATERFORD
CORK

Left

The double lens of the Fastnet lighthouse: these ladders, handles and handrails indicate that the keepers also had to be expert climbers to reach the top of their wave-lashed tower, 49 metres (160 feet) above the sea.

A motor boat can cross the North Channel almost as fast as a high-speed train crosses the English Channel; the coasts of Scotland and Northern Ireland may resemble each other, but their realities are worlds apart. By keeping due west, sailors avoid Rathlin Island, with its three lighthouses (Rathlin East, the first and tallest, was built in 1856). The green sector of the Inishowen lighthouse lies to starboard, as boats enter Lough Foyle and the splendid bay leading to the port of Londonderry.

Ireland during the time of the Celtic monks was not a warfaring land. The monks were busy spreading the Gospel and founding abbeys. The Viking invasions of the eighth century were a mere disturbance; disaster struck from the least expected quarter: Rome. In the twelfth century, Pope Adrian gave the English this island, which was considered unimportant because, viewed from the Holy See, it didn't look nearly as large as it really is (two-thirds the size of England itself). When the English fell out with Rome, Catholic Ireland became involved in eight centuries of revolt and fierce repression. These were hardly ideal conditions for development: while the economies in other European countries were growing, Ireland lagged seriously behind. Yet it had so much potential, with a central plain of great agricultural wealth and so many natural harbours: Lough Foyle, Donegal, Galway and Bantry bays, and the southern port of Cork. Without the promise of industries or local products, no one chose to sail along this jagged Atlantic coast. Ships coming from the south and heading for the Baltic entered the English Channel, then the North Sea. Those heading for Liverpool and Scotland used St. George's Channel and the Irish Sea. Limerick, at the head of the Shannon estuary, the northern-European port closest to America, might have become another Le Havre or Bordeaux—but it didn't have the prosperous hinterland or flourishing economy. So Ireland, which is ten times larger than Corsica, had only two important ports for many long years: Cork, which played a crucial role in the Middle Ages in British trading with the south (Aquitaine, Spain, Portugal); and Dublin, facing Liverpool and Wales.

In such an economic wasteland, the construction of lighthouses did not appear to be a priority, and in hindsight the process of setting up a responsible authority looks like an administrative farce. In 1740, the Englishman James Palmer was granted a patent to construct all the lights in the port of Dublin and to receive all consequent profits; the port authority was naturally most displeased. In 1767, the building and management of Irish lighthouses and pilots was entrusted to the Commissioners for Barracks, dominated by English infantry officers. In 1786, a Commission of Irish Lights was created, but responsibility for the lights was entrusted to the Customs authorities, which represented the central government. These customs officers promptly put their energy into embezzling funds, rather than building lighthouses. The guilty parties were punished, and responsibility for the lighthouses along the 300 or so kilometres of coast was transferred to the Port of Dublin, also known as the Ballast Board,[1] a name appropriate to its weight and inertia. On 24 November, 1847, the *London Times* published the following letter concerning a ship-

wreck on Fastnet rock. "And so a noble ship has perished, with its gallant captain and eighty-nine passengers, victims of the incompetence and apathy of the Ballast Board." Relatively quickly (some twenty years later), the Commissioners of Irish Lights decided to commission the Fastnet lighthouse.

With the exception of a brief period of dynamism on the part of the Ballast Board, around 1825-1835, lighthouses were built slowly. But over a period of one hundred years, lights went up around the coast and, with the exception of Fastnet, Inishtearaght and Bull Rock, the whole coastline was finally fairly well beaconed. Leaving Lough Foyle and travelling past Malin Head, sailors reach the islet of Inishtrahull, which was already here before Ireland emerged. This rock of pink gneiss was part of the tip of Greenland, together with the Scottish islands of Islay and Colonsay, and then moved eastward as the plates separated. This was 1.8 billion years ago. Yet the Inishtrahull lighthouse is the most recent in the north of the Atlantic Rim. The small tower built in 1812 was replaced by a concrete unit in 1958: the newest lighthouse, on the most ancient of lands.

"And so a noble ship has perished, with its gallant captain and eighty-nine passengers, victims of the incompetence and apathy of the Ballast Board."

A little lighthouse on piles in Lough Foyle, to the north of Ireland.

Continuing south-west, we reach Fanad Head, designed (like the first Inishtrahull lighthouse) by George Halpin, engineer to the Ballast Board. It took a shipwreck to rouse the Board's apathetic members—a shipwreck whose sole survivor was the ship's parrot (it wore a silver collar with the name of the ship, *Saldana*). Fanad Head was inaugurated on St Patrick's Day, 1817. After Fanad, boats once sailed with extreme caution: this is the "Bloody Foreland"— not named for its glorious sunsets. Tory Island is the farthest out to sea, and its first inhabitants were pirates and wreckers (the former sank ships at sea; the latter waited for the reefs to do their dirty work). The islanders can point out the Cursing Stones, where nineteenth-century Torians went to curse the *Wasp,* the gunboat that arrived with the tax-collectors (needless to say, the *Wasp* went down with all her crew). George Halpin built a lighthouse at the tip of Tory Island in 1832. In good weather, all seems calm on this bucolic-looking site, flanked by its black and white candle—until a storm comes rushing from the coasts of America, tearing up trees and bushes and everything in its path. If the keepers were not protected by the surrounding walls, they, too, would be blown away like wisps of straw.

Twenty miles farther south is Aran Island, the second of this name (the first Arran is in the Firth of Clyde, in Scotland). Neither of these two is as well-known as the third Aran, which we shall discuss later. Yet this rocky mass which guards the west of Donegal does not

The pink gneiss island of Inishtrahull was part of Greenland before Ireland emerged from the sea.

45

The entrance to the port of Cork at night;
the lighthouse and light beacons create a path of light for ships

Tory Island is one of the poorest places in Ireland.

deserve such anonymity: in 1798, its reefs were fearsome enough to justify the construction of the Aranmore light. This tower was abandoned when George Halpin inaugurated the Tory Island lighthouse, but as the new light was insufficient to beacon the entire section of this coastline, George Halpin Junior built a new Aranmore lighthouse in 1864. The Halpins, father and son, were the Irish counterparts of the Scottish Stevensons. England also had a dynasty of lighthouse builders: the Douglasses (see the following chapter). The Anglo-Saxons seem to have handed down a taste for lighthouses and odysseys from father to son. And while we can now survey them from the comfort of an armchair, it is worthwhile remembering they did it powered only by the strength of the rowers' arms, on uncharted, treacherous waters spiked with reefs.

Farther down the coast of Donegal is the westernmost tip: the islet of Rathlin O'Birne. Halpin Senior built a lighthouse there, which was completed in 1846. This was during the Ballast Board's particularly somnolent phase, and the light did not shine until ten years after it was constructed. Today, it is equipped with an isotopic generator: it is the only European lighthouse to have its own miniature nuclear power station. Moving on diagonally across the Bay of Donegal (the flash on the port side, every five seconds, is the light of Black Rock Sligo), we reach Eagle Island.

Of all the Irish lighthouses, this one is famous for withstanding the most storms; the waves climb the 60-metre (197-foot) cliff, and are still strong enough to shake walls one metre (3 feet) thick or break windows in the lantern, as they did in 1861. During a storm that year, waves flooded the lighthouse from top to bottom. The keepers couldn't get into the tower: the door opened inwards, and the water pressure was so great against the door frame that the keepers had to drill holes in the door

Eagle Island towers 67 metres (220 feet) above the waves, yet they still managed to smash its lens.

to let the water drain out. By 1835, George Halpin had built two aligned towers; in 1894, the second one was also flooded by a 60-metre (197-foot) wave, and the interior was so badly damaged that the lighthouse had to be abandoned.

Eagle Island may be the most battered lighthouse, but Black Rock Mayo, on top of a peak even steeper than Muckle Flugga to the north of Scotland, is the most inaccessible. It's a dark, sinister rock, a perfect backdrop for a remake of Dante's *Inferno*. But families lived there and children were born there: it was so difficult to ensure regular relief crews that keepers and their families lived permanently on Black Rock Mayo from 1864 to 1893. One wonders what kind of misery and deprivation can have motivated families to live in such desolation, like voluntary prisoners at the world's end?

Heading south, we come across rocks and lighthouses, each more desolate than the last, from Slyne Head, on the island of Oileanaimid (a misleading name, as there are no trees on this "isle of woods"), to Eeragh and Inisheer, which frame the Aran Islands (third of the name). The film *Man of Aran*, a poignant documentary about the islanders' impoverished lifestyle, made them famous. Poor they may be, but the islanders have designed one of the world's most seaworthy skiffs. The *curragh* is a small boat made of wood and canvas, rather similar to the Eskimo *umiak*, perfect for these rough waters. The "men of Aran" knew nothing of birthright; land was divided equally among all descendants, resulting in an extraordinary parcelling that can be seen around the Inisheer lighthouse, where every acre is walled, forming a bizarre mosaic of plants and stones.

Halfway down the coastline (past Limerick, at the head of the Shannon estuary) appear what look to be huge teeth on the horizon. The three largest each have a lighthouse on top: Inishtaraght, Skellig and Bull Rock. The latter is accompanied by the Cow, Calf and Heifer Rocks: a black and foaming herd best left unexplored. From Inishtrahull in the north to here is some 600 kilometres (400 miles). This is farther into the Atlantic than any European land; and now our route brings us back eastwards, past the Fastnet lighthouse, the Irish counterpart to Skerryvore and Eddystone. Before the Fastnet lighthouse went up, a light already existed at the top of Cape Clear, at a height of 137 metres (450 feet)—so high that it disappeared in the fog. When the *Stephen Whitney* was shipwrecked, with nearly one hundred victims, George Halpin Senior hastened to build a type of cast-iron scaffolding, 27.74 metres (91 feet) high, on Fastnet rock, with a house for the keepers 30 metres (98 feet) away. Unfortunately, the waves tore blocks of rock from the reef and were sometimes so violent that the keepers could not get from their house to the lighthouse. The tower was reinforced and a shelter was added for the men. In 1881, an exceptionally high wave smashed the lantern (the same storm carried off the top of a similar lighthouse a few miles away), and it was a miracle that the keepers survived. The structure was reinforced once more, though without much hope. Finally, in 1891, a decision was taken to build a real lighthouse. The Halpin family had died out, so the job was given to the last member of the English dynasty, William Douglass. The real hero of Fastnet, however, is James Kavanagh, a one-time mason turned foreman. Kavanagh not only fitted the 2,074 granite blocks himself, he was also the cornerstone of a team that endured terrible storms. During the four years of building, they only twice

"Fastnet" means "farewell" in ancient Celtic.

managed to work five straight days in a row. Sometimes the whole team was trapped for two to three weeks at a time in dreadfully overcrowded conditions. The foreman worked harder than anyone; he died of his exertions, just before the inauguration of the new lighthouse on 27 June 1904.

Less than eight years later, in April 1912, a brand new liner, the *Titanic,* sailed past the rock, though probably few passengers on board knew that "Fastnet" means "farewell" in ancient Celtic. Fastnet has become more than a lighthouse: it is now a famous "seamark." Participants in the Mini-Transat race here, the Figaro racers pass it on their way to call at Kinsale, and, above all, hundreds of participants in the Fastnet Race sail around it on their way from Cowes. This race (created in 1925) was the world's longest for many years—until Colonel Hasler (one of the participants) decided that 605 miles was not enough and invented the single-handed transatlantic crossing, the forerunner of all the great races: the Route du Rhum, Figaro, Whitbread, Mini-Transat, Vendée-Globe. Throughout the years, the Fastnet lighthouse has become inseparable from modern sailing.

After rounding Fastnet, the competitors head south-east, missing the lighthouses of Galley Head and Old Head Kinsale, as well as the Ballycotton lighthouse, painted black to stand out against a clear sky. Nor do they pass by the Hook Head lighthouse, built in AD 810 at the entrance to Cork, and counterpart of another venerable watchman 1,000 kilometres (600 miles) farther south: the Torre de Hércules at La Coruña.

(1) So-called because it administered the sale of ballast to ships that sailed empty (since Ireland exported less than she imported), and which needed stabilising with wood chips, gravel, etc.

The islet of Fastnet, a famous landmark for yachtsmen in ocean races.

Inishowen

Inishowen marks the approach
to Londonderry. An old lighthouse
(to the left, near the houses)
houses a foghorn. Although the
lighthouse is automated,
it has not been deserted: taxi drivers
now live in the former homes of
the lighthouse keepers.

Region - County Donegal
Position - 55°13'6"N - 6°55'7"W
Year of construction - 1837, 1871
Engineer - George Halpin Senior
Base raised by J. S. Sloane
Height - 23 metres/75 feet
Height above sea level - 28 metres/91 feet
Date of automation - 1979
Visibility - 18 miles white, 14 miles red and green
Optics - Fresnel
Lights - 2 flashes. 10 seconds
Foghorn - 2 signals. 30 seconds
Helipad - No
Open to the public - No
Inhabited - Yes

Inishtrahull

On Inishtrahull, a new lighthouse has replaced an older one that was located at the other end of the island. Every three weeks, the keeper, Donal O'Sullivan (now retired), flys in by helicopter to carry out maintenance. He knows this lighthouse better than anyone else, and in these remote parts expertise is too valuable to be left unused.

Region - County Donegal
Position - 55°25'8"N - 7°14'6"W
Year of construction - 1813, 1958
Engineer - The Collen brothers
Height - 23 metres/75 feet
Height above sea level -
59 metres/194 feet
Date of automation - 1987
Visibility - 25 miles
Optics - Fresnel
Lights - 3 white flashes. 15 seconds
Helipad - Yes
Open to the public - No
Inhabited - No

Region - County Donegal
Position - 55°16'6"N - 7°37'9"W
Year of construction - 1817
Engineer - George Halpin Senior
Height - 22 metres/72 feet
Height above sea level -
39 metres/128 feet

Date of automation - 1978
Visibility - 18 miles white, 14 miles red
Optics - Fresnel
Lights - 5 flashes. 20 seconds
Helipad - Yes
Open to the public - No
Inhabited - Yes

Fanad Head

Fanad Head was constructed by Georges Halpin. Initially only of minor importance, Fanad Head is now a helicopter base for maintenance jobs on all the lighthouses in Northern Ireland. Donal Coyle lives here with his wife and children; although he works in town, he monitors the condition of the equipment.

Tory Island

Tory Island reached its lowest point in the late Middle Ages, when piracy was rampant: this is where the Blood Coast began. The walls surrounding the lighthouse were constructed so that the lighthouse keepers would not be carried off by the winds during storms. John Joseph Doherty's face is marked by the many storms he has seen.

Region - County Donegal
Position - 55°16'4"N - 8°14'9"W
Year of construction - 1832
Engineer - George Halpin Senior
Height - 27 metres/88 feet
Height above sea level - 40 metres/131 feet
Date of automation - 1990
Visibility - 27 miles
Optics - Fresnel
Lights - 4 white flashes. 30 seconds
Helipad - Yes
Open to the public - No
Inhabited - No

Region - County Donegal
Position - 55°00'9"N - 8°33'6"W
Year of construction - 1798
Engineer - George Halpin Junior
Height - 23 metres/75 feet
Height above sea level -
71 metres/233 feet
Date of automation - 1976
Visibility - 29 miles
Optics - Fresnel
Lights - 2 white flashes. 20 seconds
Helipad - No
Open to the public - No
Inhabited - No

Aranmore

Like Tory Island, Aranmore has walls
protecting the lighthouse enclosure. When
we planned to go there, the storm was
too strong for the weekly ferry to leave port.
The first lighthouse at Aranmore was
abandoned when Tory Island was constructed.
But one light on this coast was not sufficient,
so a new tower was built in 1864.

Region - County Donegal
Position - 54°39'8"N - 8°49'9"W
Year of construction - 1856
Engineer - George Halpin Senior
Height - 20 metres/66 feet
Height above sea level - 35 metres/115 feet
Date of automation - 1974
Visibility - 18 miles
Optics - Fresnel
Lights - 1 white flash. 30 seconds
Helipad - Yes
Open to the public - No
Inhabited - No

Rathlin O'Birne

Rathlin O'Birne was the only nuclear-powered light in the world (isotope generator). Due to pressure from environmentalists, Rathlin O'Birne is now electrically powered, but remains one of the most modern lighthouses in Ireland.

Region - County Mayo
Position - 54°17'0"N - 10°05'5"W
Year of construction - 1835
Engineer - George Halpin Senior
Height - 11 metres/36 feet
Height above sea level - 67 metres/220 feet
Date of automation - 1988
Visibility - 23 miles
Optics - Fresnel
Lights - 3 white flashes. 10 seconds
Helipad - Yes
Open to the public - No
Inhabited - No

Eagle Island

In 1861, waves crashing 220 feet high around Eagle Island broke the lighthouse's lantern. So much water flooded into the tower that the door was blocked by the water pressure. The lighthouse keepers had to drill holes through it to let the water run out before they could even assess the extent of the damage. Note the enormous shield (5 feet thick) in the photograph below; it was constructed to protect the lighthouse against storms.

Black Rock Mayo

At one time, when keepers lived here with their families, children were born and grew up on Black Rock (Mayo); three months could go by between visits from the outside. Bottom left: a helicopter brings gas supplies; Black Rock was the last Irish lighthouse to be electrified (under the supervision of attendant Noel Gaughan, center).

Region - County Mayo
Position - 54°04'0"N - 10°19'2"W
Year of construction - 1864
Engineer - George Halpin Senior
Height - 15 metres/49 feet
Height above sea level - 86 metres/282 feet
Date of automation - 1974
Visibility - 22 miles
Optics - Fresnel
Lights - 1 white flash. 30 seconds
Helipad - Yes
Open to the public - No
Inhabited - No

Slyne Head

Region - County Galway
Position - 53°24'0"N - 10°14'0"W
Year of construction - 1836
Engineer - George Halpin
Height - 24 metres/79 feet
Height above sea level - 35 metres/115 feet
Date of automation - 1990
Visibility - 24 miles
Optics - Revolving light with parabolic reflectors
Lights - 2 white flashes. 15 seconds
Helipad - Yes
Open to the public - No
Inhabited - No

Slyne Head, on Oileanaimid Island,
is painted black for better visibility
in the fog (but thousands of birds
have crashed into it). We spent
two days here, sharing the last days of
Sean Faherty before his retirement. We
had such a good time together that he
gave us his uniform and his Keeper of
Irish Lights hat!

Straw Island

Inisheer

Region - County Galway
Position - 53°02'8"N - 9°31'5"W
Year of construction - 1857
Engineer - George Halpin Junior
Height - 34 metres/111 feet
Height above sea level - 34 metres/111 feet
Date of automation - 1978
Visibility - 20 miles white , 16 miles red
Optics - Fresnel
Lights - Intermittent 12 seconds
Helipad - No
Open to the public - No
Inhabited - No

Eeragh

Region - County Galway
Position - 53°08'9"N - 9°51'4"W
Year of construction - 1857
Engineer - George Halpin Junior
Height - 31 metres/102 feet
Height above sea level -
35 metres/115 feet
Date of automation - 1978
Visibility - 23 miles
Optics - Revolving light with reflectors
Lights - 2 white flashes. 15 seconds
Helipad - Yes
Open to the public - No
Inhabited - No

The Aran Islands are a world unto their own—particularly the inheritance laws, which have created an unbelievably complex patchwork of land ownership (right: on Inisheer and the abandoned Inishmore). The Eeragh lighthouse (left) has been automated with halogen lights (top). Ciaran Powell, the new attendant for the Aran Islands lighthouses, wrote his name in the first chunk of concrete that was poured (far left). To reach the small Inishmore lighthouse (top left), you have to wait for low tide, so that the helipad is out of water!

Aran Islands

Loop Head

Region - County Clare
Position - 52°33'7"N - 9°55'9"W
Year of construction - 1670, 1802, 1854
Engineer - George Halpin Senior
Height - 23 metres/75 feet
Height above sea level -
84 metres/276 feet

Date of automation - 1991
Visibility - 23 miles
Optics - Fresnel
Lights - 4 white flashes. 20 seconds
Helipad - No
Open to the public - No
Inhabited - Yes

Loop Head is situated at the tip of
an extremely long peninsula, which stretches
70 kilometres (43 miles) into the sea.
The buildings resemble a schoolhouse
or a solitary military barracks. Reflecting
bars on the tower (bottom left) keep
birds, stunned by the light, from flying into
the lantern.

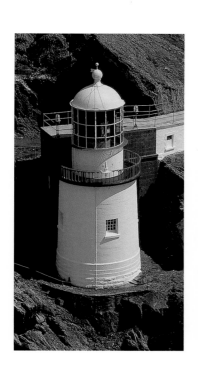

Inishtearaght

Inishtearaght would be the lighthouse on the sheerest piece of land if it weren't for Skellig (following page). The tracks of the funicular can be seen to the right of the lighthouse; it was used to bring in supplies and equipment. When the families complained of a lack of fresh meat and produce, they were allowed to raise goats.

Region - County Kerry
Position - 52°04'5"N - 10°39'7"W
Year of construction - 1870
Engineer - J.S. Sloane
Height - 17 metres/56 feet
Height above sea level - 84 metres/276 feet

Date of automation - 1956
Visibility - 27 miles
Optics - Fresnel
Lights - 2 white flashes. 20 seconds
Helipad - Yes
Open to the public - No
Inhabited - No

Skellig

Skellig is a forbidding piece of rock.
It was conquered in several stages: the first
structure was a monastery in the sixth
century (bottom right and left), followed by
a first lighthouse (centre left) no longer in
use and finally today's lighthouse, reached
by a path that zigzags around the cliffs.

Region - County Kerry
Position - 51°46'2"N - 10°32'5"W
Year of construction - 1826, 1967
Engineer - A.D.H. Martin
Height - 12 metres/39 feet
Height above sea level - 53 metres/174 feet
Date of automation - 1987
Visibility - 27 miles
Optics - Fresnel
Lights - 3 white flashes. 10 seconds
Helipad - Yes
Open to the public - No
Inhabited - No

Bull Rock

After Inishtearaght and Skellig, Bull Rock is the last in the trilogy of unscalable rocks. Bull Rock is part of a group of four islands; the others are called "Calf Island", "Cow Island" and "Oxen Island". A natural tunnel cuts through the island—but who could be surprised by this type of geological phenomenon in a place so wild it almost makes you believe in elves and fairies?

Region - County Cork
Position - 51°35'5"N - 10°18'1"W
Year of construction - 1889
Engineer - William Douglass
Height - 15 metres/49 feet
Height above sea level -
83 metres/272 feet
Date of automation - 1991
Visibility - 21 miles
Optics - Revolving light with reflectors
Lights - 1 white flash. 15 seconds
Helipad - Yes
Open to the public - No
Inhabited - No

Fastnet

Fastnet is certainly the most famous of all the Irish lighthouses, and not only because of the famous Fastnet race. In April 1912, this tower, planted on a solitary rocky outcrop, was the last view of land seen by the passengers of a brand-new, luxurious ocean liner—the *Titanic*—before it set out to sea. In ancient Celtic, Fastnet means "farewell."

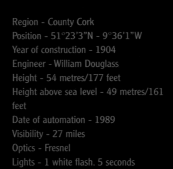

Region - County Cork
Position - 51°23'3"N - 9°36'1"W
Year of construction - 1904
Engineer - William Douglass
Height - 54 metres/177 feet
Height above sea level - 49 metres/161 feet
Date of automation - 1989
Visibility - 27 miles
Optics - Fresnel
Lights - 1 white flash. 5 seconds
Foghorn - 4 signals. 30 seconds
Helipad - Yes
Open to the public - No
Inhabited - No

Fastnet

Dick O'Briscoll has spent twenty years at Fastnet. Since the light was automated, he comes to inspect it every three weeks. When he arrives, he opens the door, which is locked up as tightly as a safe, then winds and resets the clock. He then checks the two machine rooms, inspects the generators and climbs the narrow vertical passageway housing the various equipment rooms. The base of the old lighthouse can be seen from the terrace, while the horizon seems to stretch to infinity.

Old Head Kinsale

Old Head Kinsale serves as a backdrop for a golf course (unless it's the other way around). According to legend, the first light here was not intended to save sailors, but to steer them off course—and then salvage their shipwrecked cargo. It marks the entrance to Kinsale, a lovely port famous for fishing and, at one time, its smuggling operations.

Region - County Cork
Position - 51°36'3"N - 8°31'9"W
Year of construction - 1853
Engineer - George Halpin Senior
Height - 30 metres/102 feet
Height above sea level - 72 metres/236 feet
Date of automation - 1987
Visibility - 25 miles
Optics - Fresnel
Lights - 2 white flashes. 10 seconds
Foghorn - 3 signals. 45 seconds
Helipad - No
Open to the public - No
Inhabited - Yes

Ballycotton

Ballycotton is a film set waiting
for a director: the island, just off
the Irish coast, would be a perfect
setting for an Agatha Christie mystery.
The black lighthouse, standing
within a square stone enclosure,
is marvelously sinister, and its red
light, perfectly blood-red.

Region - County Waterford
Position - 51°49'5"N - 7°59'1"W
Year of construction - 1851
Engineer - George Halpin Senior
Height - 15 metres/49 feet
Height above sea level - 59 metres/194 feet
Date of automation - 1992
Visibility - 21 miles white, 17 miles red
Optics - Spots
Lights - 1 white and red flash. 10 seconds
Foghorn - 4 signals. 90 seconds
Helipad - Yes
Open to the public - No
Inhabited - No

Hook Point

Region - County Wexford
Position - 52°07'3"N - 6°55'7"W
Year of construction - 1172
Height - 35 metres/118 feet
Height above sea level -
46 metres/151 feet
Date of automation - 1996
Visibility - 23 miles
Optics - Fresnel
Lights - 1 flash. 3 seconds
Foghorn - 2 signals. 45 seconds
Helipad - No
Open to the public - No

The oldest lighthouse in Ireland is the Hook Point Tower, constructed in AD 810. It was raised higher several times, but the thickness of the walls testifies to its great old age. Tucks Tweedy, who was the keeper, now works elsewhere, but he returns regularly to keep his former post in perfect working order.

Tuskar Rock

The Tuskar Rock lighthouse
was constructed in 1815 after
a shipwreck in which ten
people drowned on the rocks.
Some of the survivors helped
construct a tower on the flat rock
that almost claimed all their lives.
The square buildings resemble
a blockhouse; they must withstand
the fury of the sea, which lashes
over the reef.

Region - County Wexford
Position - 52°12'2"N - 6°12'4"W
Year of construction - 1815
Engineer - George Halpin Senior
Height - 34 metres/111 feet
Height above sea level - 33 metres/108 feet
Date of automation - 1993
Visibility - 24 miles
Optics - Fresnel
Lights - 2 flashes. 7.5 seconds
Foghorn - 4 signals. 45 seconds
Helipad - Yes
Open to the public - No
Inhabited - No

Mizen Head

Region - County Cork	Date of automation - 1993
Position - 51°26'9"N - 9°49'2"W	Visibility - 15 miles
Year of construction - 1909, 1959	Optics - Fresnel
Engineer - C.W. Scott	Lights - White intermittent. 4 seconds
Height - 1 metre/3 feet	Helipad - No
Height above sea level -	Open to the public - Yes (museum)
55 metres/180 feet	Inhabited - No

These are the lighthouses of Ireland, with their black or white, squat or slender towers—all built to protect sailors from the reefs, the raging seas, the fog and the storms.

Galley Head

Region - County Cork	Visibility - 23 miles
Position - 51°31'7"N - 8°57'1"W	Optics - Fresnel
Year of construction - 1878	Lights - 5 white flashes. 20 seconds
Engineer - J.S. Sloane	Foghorn - 4 signals. 30 seconds
Height - 21 metres/69 feet	Helipad - No
Height above sea level -	Open to the public - No
51 metres/167 feet	Inhabited - No
Date of automation - 1997	

Roche's Point

Region - County Cork	Visibility - 20 miles white, 16 miles red
Position - 51°47'6"N - 8°15'3"W	Optics - Revolving light with reflector
Year of construction - 1817, 1835	Lights - 1 white and red flash. 3 sec.
Engineer - George Halpin Senior	Foghorn - 1 signal. 30 seconds
Height - 15 metres/49 feet	Helipad - No
Height above sea level -	Open to the public - No
30 metres/98 feet	Inhabited - No
Date of automation - 1995	

Mine Head

Region - County Waterford	Date of automation - 1973
Position - 51°59'6"N - 7°35'2"W	Visibility - 28 miles
Year of construction - 1851	Optics - Fresnel
Engineer - George Halpin Senior	Lights - 4 white flashes. 20 seconds
Height - 21 metres/69 feet	Helipad - No
Height above sea level -	Open to the public - No
87 metres/285 feet	Inhabited - No

Dunree Fort

Region - County Donegal
Position - 54°11'9"N - 7°33'2"W
Year of construction - 1876
Engineer - J. S. Sloane
Height - 6 metres/20 feet
Height above sea level -
46 metres/151 feet

Date of automation - 1927
Visibility - 12 miles white, 9 miles red
Optics - Fresnel
Lights - 2 flashes. 5 seconds
Helipad - No
Open to the public - No
Inhabited - Yes

Crookhaven

Region - County Cork
Position - 51°28'6"N - 9°42'2"W
Year of construction - 1843
Engineer - George Halpin Senior
Height - 14 metres/46 feet
Height above sea level -
20 metres/66 feet

Date of automation - 1920s
Visibility - 13 miles white, 11 miles red
Optics - Fresnel
Lights - 1 flash, 8 seconds long
Helipad - No
Open to the public - No
Inhabited - Yes

Ardnakinna

Region - County Cork
Position - 51°37'1"N - 9°55'0"W
Year of construction - 1850, 1965
Engineer - George Halpin Senior
Height - 20 metres/66 feet
Height above sea level -
62 metres/203 feet

Date of automation - 1965
Visibility - 17 miles white, 14 miles red
Optics - Fresnel
Lights - 2 flashes. 10 seconds
Helipad - No
Open to the public - No
Inhabited - No

Black Rock Sligo

Region - County Sligo
Position - 54°18'4"N - 8°37'0"W
Year of construction - 1835
Engineer - George Halpin Senior
Height - 25 meters / 82 feet
Height above sea level - 24 m. / 79 f.
Date of automation - 1934

Visibility - 13 miles
Optics - Fresnel
Lights - 1 white flash. 5 seconds
Helipad - No
Open to the public - No
Inhabited - No

Wales and Cornwall

The Gates of Trade and Industry

Any ship from Ireland, Aquitaine, Spain, Portugal or points farther approaches the English coast via the Scilly Islands. On 22 October 1707, Sir Clowdishley Shovell, admiral of the fleet, was returning with his ships from a victorious battle against the French, which took place south of Spain. His fleet had been sailing through fog for twelve days, and his officers estimated their position well to the west of Ouessant— too far west, in fact. An ordinary seaman calculated that the route they were following would drive the ships onto the Scillies. He boldly informed Sir Clowdishley of his fears, and the admiral, outraged by such impudence, had this meddling sailor hanged for insubordination. Shortly afterwards, his ship and two others were shattered against the Scilly Islands. Two thousand British sailors lost their lives. There were only two survivors, one of whom was the admiral himself, who managed to reach the beach more dead than alive. An islander spotted the unconscious officer—and the emerald he wore on his finger—and she killed him to steal the jewel. Imagine, in the background, the roar of the surf, the splintering sounds of the ships smashing on the rocks and the masts falling, the cries of the drowning. And then imagine the final scene, thirty years later, when the sinner confessed her crime on her deathbed, producing the emerald as proof. Why do some novelists bother to invent horror stories, when maritime history provides abundant inspiration?[1] On any map of maritime horrors, the Scilly Islands would have pride of place.

SOUTH BISHOP

SMALLS

SKOKHOLM

ST ANN'S HEAD

WALES

CARDIFF

BRISTOL

NORTH LUNDY

SOUTH LUNDY

HARTLAND POINT

TREVOSE HEAD

CORNWALL

GODREVY

PENDEEN

SEVEN STONES

PLYMOUTH

START POINT

ST ANTHONY

EDDYSTONE

LIZARD POINT

LONGSHIP

WOLF ROCK

ROUND ISLAND

PENINNIS

BISHOP ROCK

CHANNEL

LES CASQUETS

LES HANOIS

Left

For a sailor, Start Point is the ideal vision of a green and pleasant land, misty but welcoming, with its trees, winding road, solid houses—and lighthouse.

Bishop Rock: the Douglass dynasty worked here for forty years.

The first light on the Scillies dates from 1680, on the island of St Agnes. It was clearly insufficient. What was needed was a beacon to signal the presence of the Scillies and of the awesome Bishop Rock reef, at their westernmost tip. This reef, submerged by the equinoctial tides, was where the Douglass saga began. The English Douglasses were the third dynasty of lighthouse builders after the Scottish Stevensons and the Irish Halpins. They worked on Bishop Rock for forty years, although their work also took them to Ireland (Fastnet), Ceylon and the Magellan Strait. Bishop Rock formed such a narrow ridge that it seemed doubtful whether an Eddystone-style lighthouse could be perched on top of it: there was nowhere to place the "building blocks" that had made Eddystone so strong. James Walker, the Trinity House engineer, therefore decided to build a metal tower on pilings. The lantern and shelter rested on six enormous cast iron legs, bolted down into the rock and propped up with braces. Keepers reached the lantern via a central tube just wide enough for a ladder. Nicholas Douglass and his son James supervised the construction of the lighthouse; they spent two years trying to overcome the same difficulties their predecessors had encountered (notably at Bell Rock, in Scotland). By the end of the 1849 season, however, the 36.60-metre (120-foot) tower was completed. All that remained was to install the lens, but the building was swept away by a storm in February 1850. Only a few cast-iron stumps were left on Bishop Rock.

The disaster was something of a paradox: in the middle of the so-called "cast-iron age", in the days when iron constructions daringly spanned gorges and rivers, the building material of the nineteenth century failed the ultimate test of strength—offshore lighthouses. These structures required granite, the more the better. A lighthouse was anchored down to the ground by its weight; its weight

These constructions required granite, the more the better.

enabled it to withstand pressure of up to thirty-five tons to the square metre, and Bishop Rock provided another opportunity to prove it.

Bishop Rock I was gone, so engineers set out to build Bishop Rock II. It was to be constructed according to the techniques perfected by Smeaton on Eddystone and the Stevensons in Scotland. Dovetailed blocks of granite would be used to ensure the solidity of the structure. James Walker and Nicholas Douglass worked on the design together, and construction was supervised by James Douglass, Nicholas's son. The structure itself posed no particular problem; the building techniques, however, meant that labourers had to work with a pickaxe, standing up to their waists in icy water. In addition, a look-out was posted; his job was to warn the rest of the team when a particularly large wave was on its way, giving them time to cling to a rock or a fellow workman. Occasionally, one of the workmen was swept off the rock and had to be retrieved—James Douglass, in particular, excelled at this sport. It took six years to erect a 33.50-metre (110-foot) tower on Bishop Rock, but at last it was inaugurated on 1 September 1858. But this was only the beginning of its troubles.

Bishop Rock trembled alarmingly. Books fell off the bookshelves. Panes of glass 19 millimetres ($3/4$ inch) thick were shattered. The prisms of the lens were splintered. The fog bell, which hung at a height of 30 metres (98 feet), was carried away by the waves. The access ladder was ripped off. The foundations began to crack. In 1860, the terrified keepers had trouble hoisting the distress flag: the pole had been swept out to sea. In 1874, another storm broke the lens in thirty different places. Something had to be done. Nicholas Douglass suggested increasing the diameter and weight of the lighthouse by building a new, taller tower around the old one. The new version would have a bulky, cylindrical base (instead of the initial tapering foundations), which would provide extra ballast at the bottom of the tower. None of this had ever been done before, but in 1884 William T. Douglass (son of James, grandson of Nicholas) undertook this Herculean task. Work began on 25 May 1883, and five months later, William's team had managed to attach fifty-seven blocks by cutting mortises in the old blocks to attach the new ones (it was too dangerous to erect scaffolding, so the stonecutters worked suspended on ropes). The higher they rose above sea level, the faster their work progressed. During this entire time, the lighthouse continued to send out its signal every night. Finally, they reached the level of the lantern, so a temporary light had to be set up on the end of a pole, up which the keepers climbed. Bishop Rock III finally shone on 25 October 1887. The weight of the lighthouse had been increased from 2,500 to 5,720 tons, and it was 43.90 metres (144 feet) tall, 10.40 metres (34 feet) taller than its predecessor.

Bishop Rock III was a remarkable landmark; it was the last English lighthouse for ships setting out from Liverpool, Southampton or Le Havre on their way to New York. During the period between the two World Wars, it was an ideal reference point for timing the departure or arrival of the great transatlantic liners. Harold Hales, a Member of Parliament, decided to award a trophy to the fastest liner: this was a sculpture depicting Neptune, sitting counting his waves and his sheep, and an angel holding a festooned globe between the tips of her wings. On top of the globe, two figurines were shown fighting over a model of a liner with three smokestacks. In 1935, the Compagnie Générale Transatlantique was the first to win this monument of pompous art. Their liner, the *Normandie*, had completed her inaugural crossing from Bishop Rock to the bay of New York at an average speed of 29.94 knots.

Ships returning from America made landfall (the point at which they first approached land) at Bishop Rock, then continued their route either north to Bristol, Cardiff or Liverpool, or east towards Southampton or London.

In the days of Bishop Rock I and II, the northern route towards the Irish Sea was the busiest. Bristol, Cardiff and Liverpool were the main ports leading to the huge industrial basin of the Midlands, with its gloomy skies darkened by smoke from the Birmingham, Sheffield and Manchester factories. This was the birthplace of the first collieries, the first steam engines and the first industrial steel mills. In the days when England was the greatest industrial power in the world, this region was the source of Britain's manpower and wealth. The maritime route to these ports was therefore extremely

Pendeen lighthouse and its foghorns.

important and it had to be made safe. Unfortunately, the coastline was jagged and dotted with treacherous reefs: lighthouses were therefore essential to the expansion of the Midlands and to that of Great Britain as a whole. Nothing would be considered too beautiful or too expensive for such a cause.

The vicinity of the Scillies had to be beaconed first: eight major lighthouses were built (not including the Sevenstones lightship) within a radius of 80 kilometres (50 miles) east-north-east from Bishop Rock. The most impressive of these, sailing towards Liverpool after Bishop Rock, is certainly Longship. A small tower had been built there in 1795 using the Eddystone III technique. It had stood for seventy-five years, enduring the usual trials: flooding, broken panes and shattered lantern. But the time had come to build a more robust, taller lighthouse on Longship.

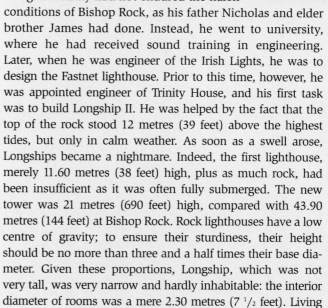

William Douglass was asked to design it. This particular member of the Douglass family had not endured the harsh conditions of Bishop Rock, as his father Nicholas and elder brother James had done. Instead, he went to university, where he had received sound training in engineering. Later, when he was engineer of the Irish Lights, he was to design the Fastnet lighthouse. Prior to this time, however, he was appointed engineer of Trinity House, and his first task was to build Longship II. He was helped by the fact that the top of the rock stood 12 metres (39 feet) above the highest tides, but only in calm weather. As soon as a swell arose, Longships became a nightmare. Indeed, the first lighthouse, merely 11.60 metres (38 feet) high, plus as much rock, had been insufficient as it was often fully submerged. The new tower was 21 metres (690 feet) high, compared with 43.90 metres (144 feet) at Bishop Rock. Rock lighthouses have a low centre of gravity; to ensure their sturdiness, their height should be no more than three and a half times their base diameter. Given these proportions, Longship, which was not very tall, was very narrow and hardly inhabitable: the interior diameter of rooms was a mere 2.30 metres (7 $^1/_2$ feet). Living there was like living in a large vertical drainpipe. Longship meant hardships, and it was therefore one of the first English light-houses to be automated.

A crew that saw the Longship light flashing to the east every ten seconds had a choice of two routes. The first, due north, led towards Liverpool. The second, to the north-east, led to the Bristol Channel and the Cornish coast, passing alongside the Pendeen lighthouse (with its compact group of buildings and its outpost with quaint-looking loudspeakers on top), and the islet of Godrevy (which is solar-powered). After Godrevy is Trevose Head (a red flash every five seconds). From this point on, the coast is clear for thirty miles or so, as far as the promontory of Hartland Point. This lighthouse, built in 1874, did not present any particular difficulties, except that an access path over half a mile long had to be carved out of the rock, and part of the mountain had to be dynamited to make it level. On a clear day, from the top of Hartland Point, the scalloped coastline of Lundy Island on the horizon is visible. In ancient Norse, *lund* means guillemot, the tiny black bird with a parrot's multicoloured beak, and the island is still a bird sanctuary

The Longships lighthouse; behind it, the Sevenstone lightship,
and left, the Round Island light.

today. It was nicknamed the "Kingdom of Heaven", after a certain Mr Heaven, who bought it in 1834. The island boasts the world's only plot of *Coincya wrightii*, a primitive—and inedible—cabbage with pretty yellow flowers.

The Severn estuary begins here. Ships following it to the end, turning right, sailing up the river Avon, entering the Avon gorge and going under the Clifton Suspension Bridge (the world's longest in 1845), reach Bristol. This is the intellectual and financial capital of the west of England. The first great iron steamship, the *Great Britain* (1845), is here. It's a little-known fact that Christopher Columbus travelled here to glean information which helped him "discover" a continent that was already well-known to Bristolian sailors.

Our route leads on past Cardiff, which was the greatest coal port in the world, towards the north of the Bristol Channel and the Welsh coast. Llwchwr is the unpronounceable name of the port in Swansea Bay. One hundred miles farther on, navigation gets more difficult. This is the easternmost tip of Wales, which ends in a mass of rocks at Skokholm, a red cliff with white striations. The lighthouse on top of it almost resembles a mosque. The next lighthouse is to the west, around the Smalls.

This group of about twenty jagged rocks has been a serious hindrance to the shipping trade, as

St Ann's Head, at the tip of Wales.

it lies right in the middle of St George's Channel, a strait between Wales and Ireland that links Liverpool and the Irish Sea with the Atlantic. This is where the *Pennsylvania* was wrecked one stormy night in 1773. The owner of the reef, a certain John Phillips, was haunted by the memory of the seventy-five victims; despite his precarious financial situation, he decided to have a lighthouse built on his rocks. He obtained a royal licence and set out to find a viable design. An improbable solution appeared with Henry Whiteside, aged twenty-six, a violin, spinet and harpsichord maker. He suggested building a wooden tower on pilings. This meant drilling holes into the rock to accommodate the nine supports. The weather conditions were so bad that by the end of the first season's work (1775), Whiteside's men had drilled a total of just one and a half holes. The following year, however, the work was more successful, and the lighthouse was finished in August 1776. It was 21.90 metres (72-feet) high and swayed frighteningly. In January of 1777, Whiteside and an assistant returned to the Smalls to reinforce the lighthouse and found themselves stranded on the reef with the three keepers, in a storm that lasted two weeks. The five of them had to live together in a mere 15 square metres (160 square feet). When they began to run out of supplies, Whiteside wrote three messages, slipped them

They started a fund, which financed the dismantling of the old tower.

into bottles and then tossed them out to sea. One of them was found on the shore, and help was sent. Whiteside then reinforced his lighthouse with fourteen extra pilings, and it stood firm. In 1801, when one of the two keepers died after an accident, his colleague put him into a makeshift coffin made out of a wardrobe, which he then secured onto the upper gallery. The raging storm burst the coffin open, and the terrified survivor found his colleague's corpse leaning nonchalantly on the railing, shroud blowing in the wind. Every night, the keeper had to see to the lantern, amid the stench of rotting flesh, but he never neglected his duty. In 1813, the lighthouse had to be reinforced, and it didn't shine all winter long (during this period, the *Fortitude* was shattered on the rocks, claiming eleven victims). In 1833, a wave demolished two of the shelter's walls, crushing the stove and the cook. Meanwhile, the founder's grandson had inherited the reef and its lighthouse, maritime trade had developed and the Smalls turned out to be a gold mine. When England decided to nationalize privately owned lighthouses in the 1830s, they had to pay £170,468 for a few rocks, a wooden lighthouse and a very profitable toll. When the wooden tower then had to be replaced, James Douglass, who had become chief engineer of Trinity House after his achievements on Bishop Rock, was asked to perform the task. Douglass had a

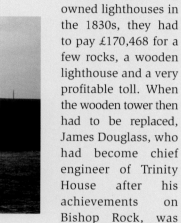

consultant, his predecessor James Walker, who had drawn up the plans for Bishop Rock. We can thank the latter for two innovations: the first was a fluted course at the base of the lighthouse, with small steps designed to decrease the strength of the waves; the second—a most welcome addition—was a lavatory. Some 150 years after Winstanley, the unforgettable lavatory-inventor and builder of Eddystone I, a rock lighthouse finally boasted a toilet. The Smalls lighthouse was built in just two years, a record, and was inaugurated on 7 August 1861. It was 43 metres (141 feet) high. The initial visibility was 15 nautical miles away, then in 1907, 17 miles (thanks to more powerful lanterns), and in 1970, it could be seen from a distance of 26 miles.

Oddly enough, the next lighthouse is called South Bishop, and is situated 230 kilometres (143 miles) north of Bishop Rock.

The lighthouse on Bishop Rock signals the English Channel route. The Channel is easily recognisable on the radar screen on the bridge of a great ship: suddenly, boats appear everywhere, arriving from the east and the south. From a maritime point of view, it's the busiest place on the planet. These ships leave great wakes in the blue-grey waters of the Channel, but they are not the only objects breaking the surface of

Eddystone IV (to the right, the base of III).

Eddystone III in its new location in Plymouth.

the water: rocks and lighthouses also leave long wakes. The Scillies come right after Bishop Rock, followed by the solitary lighthouse of Wolf Rock, creating a wake worthy of a supertanker, due to the extremely strong current. The place is so inaccessible that seventy years went by between the first design for a lighthouse and its construction by the brothers James and William Douglass. They had all kinds of mishaps. In some years, the workmen could only work on the rock for a total of two hundred hours. The building work continued for seven years. Wolf Rock was inaugurated on 1 January 1870 and was so inaccessible that, in 1973, it became the first British lighthouse to be equipped with a helipad.

Wolf Rock was the first, but many others followed including Eddystone (after Lizard Point with its strange post-Gothic double lighthouse). The father of all offshore lighthouses is unrecognisable and with good reason: Eddystone III, Smeaton's legendary tower (see Chapter I), no longer supports this helipad, but Eddystone IV, the work of James Douglass. In 1877, after 125 years of service, Smeaton's masterpiece was as good as new—but the rock on which it stood was gradually disintegrating, and a new tower had to be built. There was no more room on the rock, so an underwater cofferdam was

The lightship Channel, *one of the last of its kind still in operation.*

constructed for the new tower. Work went on for four years, and when it was finished, Eddystone IV, 51.20 metres (168 feet) high, towered over Eddystone III, which was a mere 21.30 metres (70 feet). The latter was closed down, due to the gradual erosion of the rock, and there was talk of demolishing it, but it was finally saved by the inhabitants of nearby Plymouth. They had not forgotten the lighthouse's role in their port's prosperity, and refused to see such a monument destroyed. They started a fund, which financed the dismantling of the old tower. It proved almost as difficult to dismantle this rock lighthouse block by block as it was to build a new one, and William Douglass nearly died in the process when he fell 20 metres (65 feet) onto the rocks. A wave washed up just before he hit the rocks, and the engineer lived to tell the tale and to build other lighthouses, once Eddystone III was reconstructed on Plymouth Hoe. It now overlooks the harbour from which Francis Drake, the *Mayflower* pilgrims, Francis Chichester and Eric Tabarly set sail.

After Start Point is the *Channel*, a lightship, and the ragged Alderney coastline, where the first lighthouse was set up in 1724. To the right, the double flash every five seconds is from the lighthouse of Les Hanois, built by William Douglass and James Walker in 1862. Opposite it, to the left, is a purplish line dotted with lights: this is the French coast.

South Bishop

Region - Wales
Position - 51°51'00"N - 5°25'00"W
Year of construction - 1839
Engineer - James Walker
Height - 11 metres/36 feet
Height above sea level - 44 metres/144 feet
Date of automation - 1984
Visibility - 19 miles
Optics - Fresnel
Lights - 1 white flash. 5 seconds
Foghorn - 3 signals. 45 seconds
Helipad - Yes
Open to the public - No
Inhabited - No

Contrary to what its name
may lead you to believe,
South Bishop is far to the
north of Bishop Rock!
Along with Smalls, it is
the English (or rather Welsh)
lighthouse that lies closest
to Ireland. Although it
is near the mainland, the
lighthouse nevertheless must
be autonomous, and has
large reserves of fuel for its
generators.

Smalls

The Smalls reef is isolated between Cornwall and Ireland. Stuck on the reef in 1777, the man who built the first light called for help by sending messages in a bottle—which saved him. This first wooden lighthouse was privately owned and was an extremely profitable piece of property. The current tower, which dates to 1861, was the first English lighthouse fitted out with a toilet. Visible in the top photograph are the reinforcements required for the installation of a helipad.

Region - Wales
Position - 51°43'00"N - 5°40'00"W
Year of construction - 1861
Engineer - James Walker
Height - 41 meters/135 feet
Height above sea level - 38 meters/125 feet
Date of automation - 1987
Visibility - 25 miles
Optics - Fresnel
Lights - 3 white flashes. 15 seconds
Foghorn - 2 signals. 60 seconds
Helipad - Yes
Open to the public - No
Inhabited - No

Skokholm

Skokholm island is one of the largest ornithological reserves in Europe. The lighthouse, rising up over its square base, is particularly visible from a distance. The tip of land visible to the right of the horizon in the photograph below (bottom right) is St Ann's Head.

Region - Wales
Position - 51°42'00"N - 5°17'00"W
Year of construction - 1916
Engineer - Thomas Matthews
Height - 18 metres/59 feet
Height above sea level - 54 metres/177 feet
Date of automation - 1983
Visibility - 20 miles
Optics - Fresnel
Lights - 1 red flash. 10 seconds
Foghorn - 1 signal. 10 seconds
Helipad - Yes
Open to the public - No
Inhabited - No

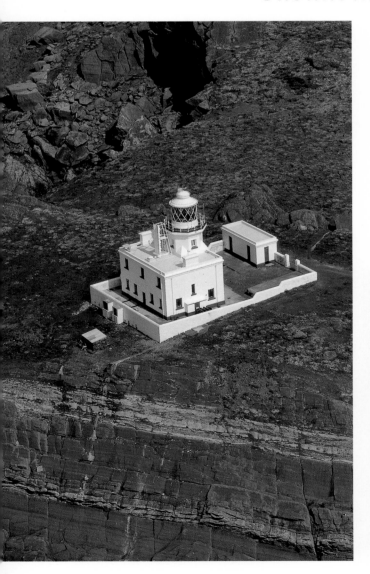

Region - Wales
Position - 51°40'83"N - 05°10'38"W
Year of construction - 1714, 1841
Height - 13 metres/43 feet
Height above sea level - 48 metres/157 feet
Date of automation - 1998
Visibility - 18 miles white, 17 miles red
Optics - Fresnel
Lights - 1 white and red flash. 5 seconds
Foghorn - 2 signals. 60 seconds
Helipad - Yes
Open to the public - No
Inhabited - No

The cliff at St Ann's Head is as
multicolored as a tapestry.
The lighthouse is a stocky yet
powerful structure: ship traffic
at this point is quite heavy.

St Ann's Head

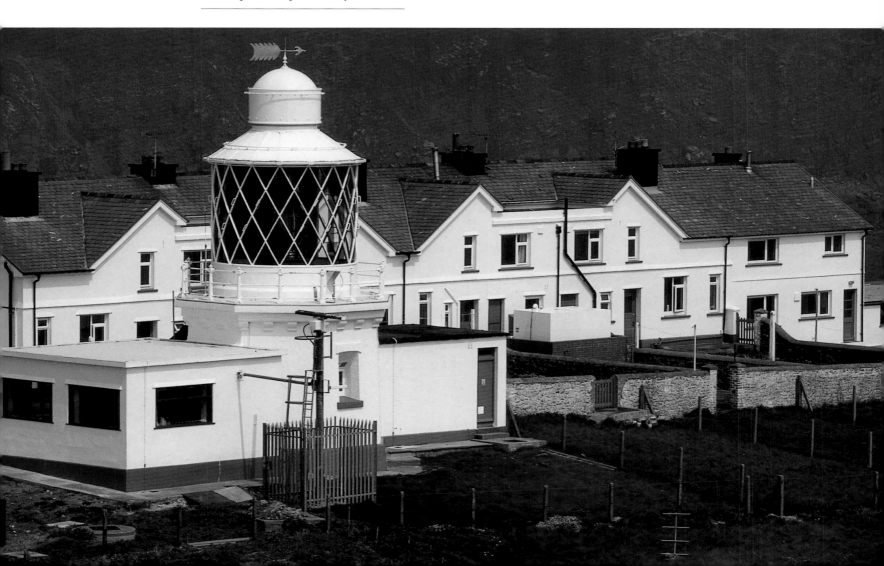

Region - Cornwall
Position - 51°12'00"N - 4°41'00"W
Year of construction - 1897
Engineer - Daniel Alexander
Height - 17 metres/56 feet
Height above sea level - 50 metres/165 feet
Date of automation - 1971
Visibility - 17 miles
Optics - Fresnel
Lights - 1 white flash. 15 seconds
Helipad - No
Open to the public - No
Inhabited - No

North Lundy

Lundy Island belonged to a certain
Mr Heavens, who nicknamed it
"Heavens Island". There are three
lighthouses on Lundy: one to the north
(Lundy North); another one, no longer
in use, in the centre (it is also pictured
on page 89, in the upper righthand
part of the bottom photograph); and
a third one in the south (Lundy South).

South Lundy

Each lighthouse has its own specific equipment: on this one (no longer in use), in the centre of the island, the lantern was replaced by a chaise longue! At the top of the short tower of Lundy North is the group of foghorns. A primitive type of cabbage, the *Coincya wrightii*, grows not far from here; this is the only place this plant can be found.

Region - Cornwall
Position - 51°10'00"N - 4°39'00"W
Year of construction - 1897
Engineer - Daniel Alexander
Height - 16 metres/52 feet
Height above sea level - 53 metres/174 feet
Date of automation - 1994
Visibility - 15 miles
Optics - Fresnel
Lights - 1 white flash. 5 seconds
Foghorn - 1 signal. 25 seconds
Helipad - Yes
Open to the public - No
Inhabited - No

Godrevy

The Godrevy lighthouse seems to be something of a sacred monument, with its hexagonal tower surrounded by a circular wall, which slants like a sun dial. Until 1942, each changing of the guard at the lighthouse meant that a keeper had to cross the channel to the island in a chair suspended from a rope, a type of (very) primitive chairlift.
A slope was constructed between the enclosure and the tower to recover rainwater. Today, the light is powered by solar panels.

Region - Cornwall
Position - 50°14'5"N - 5°23'09"W
Year of construction - 1859
Engineer - James Walker
Height - 26 metres/85 feet
Height above sea level - 37 metres/121 feet
Date of automation - 1939
Visibility - 12 miles white, 9 miles red
Optics - Fresnel
Lights - White and red flash. 10 seconds
Helipad - Yes
Open to the public - No
Inhabited - No

Round Island

The only thing round about Round Island is the lighthouse tower. This photograph shows a somewhat idyllic view: imagine these same rocks, at night during a mighty storm—they would be invisible. This gives some idea of just how dangerous the Scilly Islands (of which Round Island is the northermost point) were.

Region - Cornwall (Scilly Islands)
Position - 49°59'70''N - 06°19'33''W
Year of construction - 1887
Engineer - James Douglass
Height - 19 metres/62 feet
Height above sea level - 55 metres/180 feet
Date of automation - 1987
Visibility - 24 miles
Optics - Fresnel
Lights - 1 white flash. 10 seconds
Foghorn - 4 signals. 60 seconds
Helipad - Yes
Open to the public - No
Inhabited - No

Bishop Rock

Bishop Rock lighthouse is the third to have been
built on this reef. Bishop Rock I was swept away
before its lantern was installed. Bishop Rock II shook
far too much. Another lighthouse was therefore built
so that its weight would anchor it more solidly
to the rock. Bishop Rock was built by three members
of the Douglass family: Nicholas, father of this line
of engineers; his son, James; and his grandson,
William.

Region - Cornwall (Scilly Islands)
Position - 49°52'33"N - 06°26'70"W
Year of construction - 1858
Engineer - James Walker
Height - 49 metres/161 feet
Height above sea level - 44 metres/144
feet
Date of automation - 1992
Visibility - 24 miles
Optics - Fresnel
Lights - 2 white flashes. 15 seconds
Foghorn - 2 signals. 90 seconds
Helipad - Yes
Open to the public - No
Inhabited - No

Longship

Of all the lighthouses built on reefs, Longship is the narrowest: the inner diameter of the rooms is approximately 2.30 metres/I $^1/_2$ feet (including the space required for the ladder to climb from one floor to another). Living at Longship was like living in a vertical tube. It is not surprising that this lighthouse was dreaded by lighthouse keepers.

Region - Cornwall
Position - 50°04'00"N - 05°44'08"W
Year of construction - 1795, 1875
Engineer - James Douglass
Height - 35 metres/115 feet
Height above sea level - 35 metres/115 feet
Date of automation - 1988
Visibility - 18 miles
Optics - Fresnel
Lights - 1 white and red intermittent flash. 5 seconds
Foghorn - 1 signal. 10 seconds
Helipad - Yes
Open to the public - No
Inhabited - No

Wolf Rock

In calm weather, Wolf Rock is visible from afar because of the wide wake formed around it by the force of the tides. During storms, the 34-metre (111-feet) pillar can disappear completely in a geyser of sea mist and foam. In conditions as Dantesque as these, it is not surprising that seventy years went by between the time the first lighthouse was proposed and the time it was finally constructed.

Region - Cornwall
Position - 49°56'72"N - 5°48'50"W
Year of construction - 1870
Engineer - James Walker
Height - 41 metres/135 feet
Height above sea level - 34 metres/111 feet
Date of automation - 1988
Visibility - 23 miles
Optics - Fresnel
Lights - 1 white flash. 15 seconds
Foghorn - 1 signal. 30 seconds
Helipad - Yes
Open to the public - No
Inhabited - No

Region - Cornwall
Position - 49°57'58"N - 5°12'7"W
Year of construction - 1619, 1756
Engineer - John Killigrew
Height - 19 metres/62 feet
Height above sea level -
70 metres/230 feet
Date of automation - 1998
Visibility - 25 miles
Optics - Fresnel
Lights - 1 white flash. 3 seconds
Foghorn - 2 signals. 60 seconds
Helipad - No
Open to the public - No
Inhabited - No

Lizard Point

Lizard lighthouse is extremely simple, but its austerity is offset by the buildings surrounding it, constructed in a post-Gothic style worthy of the worst British college. This official aspect is well suited to the lighthouse used as the reference point for timing crossings of the north Atlantic.

Eddystone

The Eddystone III lighthouse (the base can be seen on page 97, to the right of Eddystone IV)
was dismantled and reconstructed at Plymouth, a move paid for by the city's residents.
This is a testimony to their attachment to the rock's most famous lighthouse,
the legendary tower constructed by Smeaton in 1759. This structure was a prototype
for every other lighthouse that followed. Both the eighteenth-century Eddystone III and
the nineteenth-century Eddystone IV remain steadfast examples of modernism. They have no decoration
whatsoever. There are no superfluous elements: it was this triumph of functional engineering
over architectural constraints that would be put to use to construct French lighthouses.

Region - Devon
Position - 50°10'80''N - 04°15'90''W
Year of construction - 1696-1698, 1708, 1759, 1882
Engineer - James Douglass
Height - 49 metres/161 feet
Height above sea level - 41 metres/135 feet
Date of automation - 1982
Visibility - 22 miles
Optics - Fresnel
Lights - 2 white flashes. 10 seconds
Foghorn - 3 signals. 60 seconds
Helipad - Yes
Open to the public - No
Inhabited - No

Eddystone

All the lighthouses on British land have been transformed to accommodate helicopters. At Eddystone IV—as at other lighthouses— a metal-braced structure was constructed to support a helipad. A trap door leads up to this platform. Equipment is carried in slings under the helicopter: three sacks, which required three flights, are visible on the platform. Below: the lighthouse's "dormitory": although the lights have been automated, maintenance operations at the lighthouse sometimes take up to several weeks. The technicians live in the same isolation as did the lighthouse keepers of old.

Start Point

Land is less stable than people thin
Eddystone III had to be replaced bec
support was cracking. The situation
worse at Start Point: the first lighthe
which was situated to the left of the
structure, was swept away by a lan
The new lighthouse had to be reinf
after the ground subsided in Decen

Region - Devon
Position - 50°13'30"N - 3°38'47"W
Year of construction - 1836
Engineer - James Walker
Height - 28 metres/91 feet
Height above sea level - 62 metres/203 feet
Date of automation - 1993
Visibility - 25 miles
Optics - Fresnel
Lights - 3 white flashes. 10 seconds
Foghorn - 1 signal. 60 seconds
Helipad - No
Open to the public - No
Inhabited - Yes

Les Casquets

Region - Channel Islands
Position - 49°43'38"N - 2°23'55"W
Year of construction - 1724
Engineer - Thomas Le Coq
Height - 14 metres/46 feet
Height above sea level - 37 metres/121 feet
Date of automation - 1990

Visibility - 24 miles
Optics - Fresnel
Lights - 5 flashes. 30 seconds
Foghorn - 2 signals. 60 seconds
Helipad - Yes
Open to the public - No
Inhabited - No

The five flashes produced every 30 seconds by Casquets lighthouse seem brighter than any others, like a brilliant magnesium flash illuminating the English Channel. Three towers existed at Casquets in 1724. Two of them have survived: one is the current lighthouse, the other is the helipad.

Hartland Point

Region - Devon
Position - 51°01'3"N - 4°31'4"W
Year of construction - 1874
Engineer - James Douglass
Height - 18 metres/59 feet
Height above sea level -
37 metres/121 feet
Date of automation - 1984

Visibility - 25 miles
Optics - Fresnel
Lights - 6 white flashes. 15 seconds
Foghorn - 1 signal. 60 seconds
Helipad - Yes
Open to the public - No
Inhabited - No

Britain, where the first modern lighthouse
was created (Eddystone III), did not restrict
designs to this style (re-created at Les Hanois).
There are also lighthouses in the middle of
fields, like Peninnis, while others are isolated
(Hartland), official (Pendeen), or are offshore
altogether, like Sevenstones and Channel.

Trevose Head

Region - Cornwall
Position - 50°32'92"N - 5°02'07"W
Year of construction - 1847
Engineer - Jacob & Thomas Olver
Height - 27 metres/88 feet
Height above sea level -
62 metres/203 feet
Date of automation - 1995

Visibility - 20 miles
Optics - Fresnel
Lights - 1 white flash. 75 seconds
Foghorn - 2 signals. 30 seconds
Helipad - No
Open to the public - No
Inhabited - Yes

Pendeen

Region - Cornwall
Position - 50°9'85"N - 5°40'20"W
Year of construction - 1900
Engineer - Sir Thomas Matthews
Height - 17 metres/56 feet
Height above sea level -
59 metres/194 feet
Date of automation - 1995

Visibility - 16 miles
Optics - Fresnel
Lights - 1 white flash. 15 seconds
Foghorn - 1 signal. 20 seconds
Helipad - No
Open to the public - From Easter to
end of September
Inhabited - Yes

Seven Stones

Region - Cornwall
Position - 50°03'58"N - 6°04'28"W
Year of construction - 1958-1967
Engineer - Philip & Son, Dartmouth
Length - 45 metres/148 feet
Height above sea level -
12 metres/39 feet
Date of automation - 1987

Visibility - 25 miles
Optics - Fresnel
Lights - 3 white flashes. 30 seconds
Foghorn - 3 signals. 30 seconds
Helipad - Yes
Open to the public - No
Inhabited - No

Peninnis

Region - Cornwall (Scilly Islands)
Position - 49°54'2"N - 6°18'2"W
Year of construction - 1911
Height - 14 metres/46 feet
Height above sea level -
36 metres/118 feet
Date of automation - 1911

Visibility - 17 miles
Optics - Fresnel
Lights - 1 white flash. 20 seconds
Helipad - No
Open to the public - No
Inhabited - No

St Anthony

Region - Wales
Position - 50°8'43"N - 5°00'90"W
Year of construction - 1835
Height - 19 metres/62 feet
Height above sea level -
22 metres/72 feet
Date of automation - 1988
Visibility - 22 miles

Lights - White and red,
occulting 15 seconds
Optics - Fresnel
Foghorn - 1 signal, 3 seconds long.
30 seconds
Helipad - No
Open to the public - No
Inhabited - Yes

Channel

Region - English Channel
Position - 49°54'42"N - 02°53'67"W
Year of construction - 1958
Engineer - Philip & Son of Dartmouth
Longueur - 45 metres/148 feet
Height above sea level -
12 metres/39 feet
Date of automation - 1989

Visibility - 25 miles
Optics - Revolving light with reflectors
Lights - 1 white flash. 15 seconds
Foghorn - 1 signal. 20 seconds
Helipad - Yes
Open to the public - No
Inhabited - No

Les Hanois

Region - Channel Islands
Position - 49°26'16"N - 2°42'06"W
Year of construction - 1862
Engineer - Nicholas Douglass
Height - 33 metres/108 feet
Height above sea level -
30 metres/98 feet
Date of automation - 1996

Visibility - 20 miles
Optics - Fresnel
Lights - 2 flashes. 13 seconds
Foghorn - 2 signals. 60 seconds
Helipad - Yes
Open to the public - No
Inhabited - No

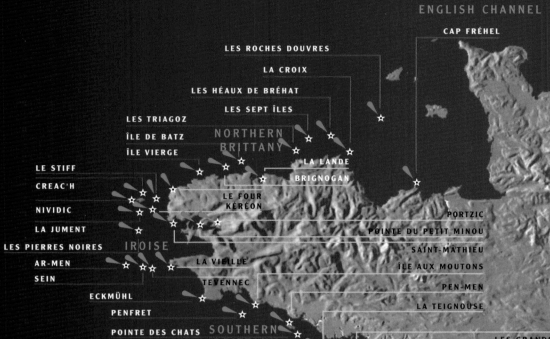

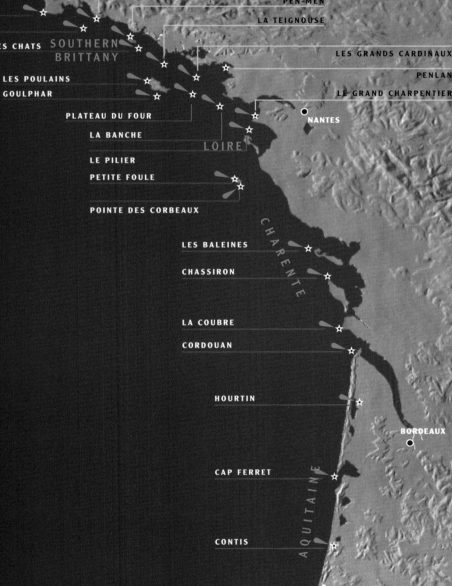

ENGLISH CHANNEL

CAP FRÉHEL

LES ROCHES DOUVRES

LA CROIX

LES HÉAUX DE BRÉHAT

LES SEPT ÎLES

LES TRIAGOZ

ÎLE DE BATZ

ÎLE VIERGE

NORTHERN BRITTANY

LA LANDE

BRIGNOGAN

LE STIFF

CREAC'H

NIVIDIC

LA JUMENT

LES PIERRES NOIRES

AR-MEN

SEIN

IROISE

LE FOUR

KÉRÉON

PORTZIC

POINTE DU PETIT MINOU

SAINT-MATHIEU

ÎLE AUX MOUTONS

PEN-MEN

LA TEIGNOUSE

LA VIEILLE

TEVENNEC

ECKMÜHL

PENFRET

POINTE DES CHATS

SOUTHERN BRITTANY

LES GRANDS CARDINAUX

PENLAN

LE GRAND CHARPENTIER

LES POULAINS

GOULPHAR

NANTES

PLATEAU DU FOUR

LA BANCHE

LOIRE

LE PILIER

PETITE FOULE

POINTE DES CORBEAUX

CHARENTE

LES BALEINES

CHASSIRON

LA COUBRE

CORDOUAN

HOURTIN

BORDEAUX

CAP FERRET

AQUITAINE

CONTIS

POINTE SAINT-MARTIN

SOCOA

BASQUE COUNTRY

eading south-east, England disappears over the horizon and Les Hanois lighthouse fades from view. Continuing south, the first French landfall is called Les Roches Douvres. This reef lies 40 kilometres (24 miles) from the nearest coast and is even more isolated than the Smalls in St George's Channel. Les Roches Douvres is Europe's most isolated lighthouse. It replaced a metal tower built in 1867, which was blown up by the Germans to hinder the Allied advance. The present-day lighthouse was built in 1948, so it is fairly recent, but it certainly doesn't look like it. It seems to be far older. It's a strange structure, surprisingly spacious in comparison to almost any lighthouse in Great Britain or Ireland. It gives an impression of great wealth and abundance. Les Roches Douvres is not, however, an isolated example: with every new reef and cape, each lighthouse is more spectacular than the last, especially after viewing the spartan, functional Anglo-Saxon towers. Almost every French lighthouse is a decorative monument, with artistic additions ranging from neo-Gothic to Baroque and Art Deco.

Left

Ar-Men

Cap Fréhel

Le Grand Jardin

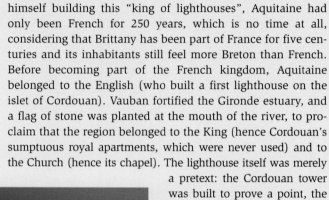
Le Four

La Vieille

The apparent luxury of the crenellated tower with superfluous galleries, located in the remotest outposts of French territory, is somewhat misleading. Some of the most beautiful French lighthouses have depended on public donors to offset lack of state funding. One example occurred in June 1997, when the keepers at Les Roches Douvres went on strike, refusing to be relieved. "We are concerned about the safety of the lighthouse…we're not doing this for pleasure, and we hope the authorities will give us a quick answer as regards the urgency of renovating this lighthouse, and do something about the 640 days overtime our colleagues have put in", they declared to the *Télégramme de Brest* newspaper. "The equipment is worn out, one of the two wind pumps has been broken down since Christmas, the windows are oozing water, the motors of the generating sets are twenty-six years old and the causeway is cracked," added the head keeper.

Les Roches Douvres

What a contrast exists between these palace-like structures and the complaints of their keepers. These lighthouses are so different from the ones in Great Britain and Ireland that they can be suspected of being French before being functional, in other words, beauty comes before duty. An examination of the towers that signal the French coastline reveals that they illuminate more than the horizon: they also shed light on the way the country works.

France's oldest existing lighthouse is at Cordouan; an older one stood at Boulogne, but it collapsed in 1644 after 1,605 years of service. It had been built on the orders of Caius Caligula and looked like a ziggurat, with twelve stepped storeys. Facing the English Channel, it stood 60-metres (197-feet) high and would still be standing, if quarriers had not been allowed to mine the cliff, which collapsed, taking the age-old tower with it in its fall. France's oldest lighthouse today is therefore Cordouan. When Louis de Foix bankrupted himself building this "king of lighthouses", Aquitaine had only been French for 250 years, which is no time at all, considering that Brittany has been part of France for five centuries and its inhabitants still feel more Breton than French. Before becoming part of the French kingdom, Aquitaine belonged to the English (who built a first lighthouse on the islet of Cordouan). Vauban fortified the Gironde estuary, and a flag of stone was planted at the mouth of the river, to proclaim that the region belonged to the King (hence Cordouan's sumptuous royal apartments, which were never used) and to the Church (hence its chapel). The lighthouse itself was merely a pretext: the Cordouan tower was built to prove a point, the only reason for its Baroque splendour.

Cordouan is rather like a cramped little Versailles, but what of the other French lighthouses? La Jument, which was as difficult to build as Skerryvore or Bishop Rock, looks like a keep straight out of the history books, although it only dates from 1904. The Héaux de Bréhat and its battlements would not look out of place in the medieval city of Carcassonne, but they were designed by the architect Léonce Raynaud (1803-1880), renowned for his aversion to ornamentation. The crenellated Four lighthouse (1874) looks more like a meticulous medieval reconstruction than a maritime edifice. Cap Fréhel, which was rebuilt after the Second World War, boasts loopholes alongside elements of a Romanesque cloister, and the latticed stairwell looks like a luxurious residential property. The tower of Île d'Yeu is an Art Deco mausoleum, and the Poulains is a church that happens to have a lantern instead of a steeple.

Why such criticism if these lighthouses work well (which is undoubtedly the case)? There are two reasons. The first is the expense of such architectural extravagance: facilities

Les Poulains

Le Stiff

Les Pierres Noires

Cordouan

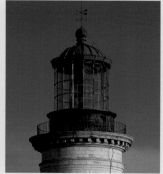

Kéréon

La Croix

Les Héaux de Bréhat

L'île Vierge

built with taxpayer's money should be designed as economically as possible (as per Anglo-Saxon style), whereas the opposite is actually the case. The second reason is that these extraordinary maritime manor houses symbolize a certain image of France, but not necessarily the one their architects had in mind.

What do these castles, bell-towers, keeps and chapels really tell us? That architecture, before being functional, must meet formal standards (preferably traditional in style). This was the credo of the Paris School of Civil Engineering, where Léonce Raynaud had taught. He wrote: "Nothing is beautiful unless it is becoming," and, in his famous treatise of 1850, prophesied utter conventionality in architecture. He and his students were responsible for building many of the French lighthouses. While Gustave Eiffel was designing the well-proportioned forms of the Garabit viaduct and the highly controversial Eiffel Tower, the Civil Engineers were building medieval-looking lighthouses, as if the Middle Ages were still the ultimate reference in aesthetics. While Le Corbusier raged: "We are trying to disguise … the ugliness of accumulation: we are obsessed with the past," the state architects were building lighthouses as monuments to past glory.

The Anglo-Saxons had built strictly utilitarian towers, designed by thrifty engineers; their buildings had the basic essentials, no frills. Their lighthouses were models of pure engineering. But in France, the cult of Beauty meant that the lighthouse was seen as a work of applied architecture, in which the picturesque prevailed over the functional. All these bastions exiled at sea, weighed down with references to a Great Military Past—battlements, loopholes and machicolations—prove that "official" beauty was quite retrograde. The crenellated keep of the Pierres Noires, facing Brest, is a surrealistic Disneyland-on-the-Sea.

What do these ornamental lighthouses contain? Staircases. French towers are usually empty, except for a spiral staircase. There was no room for lodgings,[1] so separate shelters were built for the keepers, who had to climb the

Eckmühl

stairs all the way up to their workplace (397 steps at Île Vierge, 315 at Eckmühl). British towers, on the other hand, are like vertical submarines in which keepers could move around from one chamber to another by climbing ladders, much like an engine room. They were stationary ships, whose style was in strict accordance with the constraints of the ocean: these are authentic maritime forms. Compared to the British stone vessels, French lighthouses look like extensions of dry land, little bits of countryside lacking only trees. They smell of the earth: they are landsmen's monuments.

The state-financed French Lighthouse Authority carries out a mission entrusted to it by the government. Lighthouses are not financed (as they are in Anglo-Saxon countries) by light dues levied on ships. The budget for French lighthouses is covered by general taxation, so everyone contributes, including the residents of Alsace and Auvergne, or other inland areas whose parliamentary representatives, understandably, show no great enthusiasm for the problem of beaconing the coastline.

Fortunately, other options appeared when government funding failed. Everyone found the Penmarc'h lighthouse dissatisfactory, as it was too low, but the state did not care to spend more money on this desolate spot. A donor finally appeared: Adélaïde Louise Davout, marchioness of Blocqueville, and daughter of a brigadier who was made Prince of Eckmühl following a battle. In 1885, she bequeathed 300,000 French francs for the construction of a lighthouse "on a dangerous part of the coasts of France. My old friend, Baron Baude, has often told me that there are many coves on the Brittany coast, which are still dark and dangerous. I would like the Eckmühl lighthouse to be erected there … because I wish this noble name to be long blessed." The Lighthouse Authority proved itself worthy of the bequest: it built a lighthouse-mausoleum, 65-metres (213-feet) high, and in one of its rooms is a full-size bronze of the Prince of Eckmühl.

Another gift was received from the grand-niece of Monsieur Le Dall de Kéréon, a lieutenant guillotined during the Terreur (during the French Revolution). She wanted a

Les Barges

Port Navalo

Les Triagoz

Le Grand Charpentier

The La Croix lighthouse, at the mouth of the Trieux River.

lighthouse to bear her ancestor's name, and bequeathed a sufficient sum of money to cover not only the construction of the Kéréon lighthouse (between Ouessant and Molène) but also to decorate it sumptuously, with oak panelling from Hungary and parquet inlaid with a pattern of compass cards.

In 1904, Charles-Eugène Potron bequeathed 400,000 francs to build a lighthouse "on rock, in one of the most dangerous regions of the Atlantic coast, such as the island of Ouessant." He placed one condition on his bequest, however: if the lighthouse was not working after seven years, the money would go to the Sea Rescue Society. The Paris authorities hesitated: the Créac'h lighthouse fulfilled its function, and Ar-Men had finally been completed, so was another lighthouse really necessary? However, the engineers of the Finistère region thought it was worth signalling the entrance to the Fromveur fairway (which leads directly to Brest), and their Parisian superiors bowed to this decision. Construction of the La Jument lighthouse was begun in haste, in the dramatic conditions typical of rock lighthouses. In their rush to finish in time, the engineers did not notice that the rock was split, nor that another reef sent waves crashing onto the site of the future lighthouse, nor that the base block lacked height. La Jument was fini-shed *in extremis*, but reinforcement work had to begin immediately and continued for twenty years. In the end, the tower had to be weighted down artificially, by anchoring three cables vertically underneath it, with a tension of 2,500 tons, which maintained the lighthouse on its rock.

The difficulties of building La Jument pale when compared with those of Ar-Men. The Civil Engineers could be relied upon for their remarkably bad taste, but their competence and their courage cannot be denied. Ar-Men was proof of this and will always be one of their finest achievements. It was a challenge from the outset. Lighthouses had already been built on rocks which were only visible at low tide, but never in a place where the currents could be more than eight knots. And never on a rock where no one had even managed to land. From 1860 to 1866, Léonce Raynaud had made seven unsuccessful attempts to land there. Yet a lighthouse had to be built on this reef, which was right in the middle of the Sein passage: it was essential for the safety of passing ships. In 1867, a team of eight men finally managed to land seven straight times, spending a total of eight hours on Ar-Men, during which they drilled fifteen holes. The following year the rock was cleaned up and thirty-four more holes were drilled. The stonework could begin: during the third year, the workmen embedded 25 cubic metres of blocks on the site in forty-two hours. They landed twenty-four times, but during the fourth season, could make only eight landings—and so it went, until 1881, fourteen years later. Fourteen seasons of stubborn slogging, of waiting, of frustrated endeavours, during which 404 voyages were made, with only 291 successful landings.

Jean Malgorn, head lighthouse keeper for more than twenty years at Île Vierge.

"... on the rock, in one of the most dangerous regions of the Atlantic coast, such as the island of Ouessant."

Ar-Men holds all the worst records. It took the longest to build, its living conditions were the hardest and relieving the keepers was the most perilous of operations. In 1923, the keeper, Monsieur Fouquet, was stranded there for 101 days: completely cut off from the rest of the world, he survived more than three months without fresh supplies.

Since the 1950s, lighthouse keepers have been referred to as "maintenance operatives", but they are still the only landsmen whom sailors regard as their fellows. These nautical landsmen have dynasties of their own: Jean Malgorn was keeper on Île Vierge for twenty years, together with his wife; his brother was a keeper at Cap Fréhel; his nephew at La Giraglia in Corsica. Another term for "maintenance operative" is "electro-technician", but technical competence is not enough. A keeper must also be able to withstand the solitude and the fear. Abraham, keeper at Ar-Men, wrote: "You'd have to be stupid not to be afraid in a lighthouse." Sometimes they are required to act selflessly: during a particularly violent storm, La Jument shook so badly that the optic's mercury bath overflowed and the lantern had to be turned by hand all night long, while furious waves hammered the tower. Afterwards, the drops of mercury had to be swept up, in preparation for the following night.

Antoine de Saint Exupéry did much to create the legends of the early days of the French airmail service. Lighthouses could have used their own Saint Exupéry to popularize the idea of the lantern that must be lit, come what may. Examples of devotion to duty are plentiful, and not only in such extreme places as Ar-Men or La Jument. Kerdonis is a low turret on a clifftop on Belle-Île; from 1904, its keeper was a certain Désiré Matelot. After twenty years as keeper at the isolated rock lighthouse Les Grands Cardinaux, he was offered this new position, which meant that he could live with his family at the foot of the lighthouse. In April 1911, Désiré Matelot had violent stomach pains just as he was checking the lantern mechanism. He died at 7:45 pm, when the light had to be lit—and there was no way of calling for help: Le Palais, the nearest town, was 12 kilometres (7 miles) away. Unfortunately, the dying man had not been able to wind the mechanism fully, and the lantern refused to turn. So, while the bereaved mother watched over her dead husband, her ten-year-old younger daughter went to turn the lantern by hand, until the two older children, who worked through the night, relieved her. Later, the widowed Mme Matelot, who received a pension of just 21 francs, tried to recover the 58 francs that the Administration owed her for the eighteen days her husband had worked in April. Three months later, the debt had still not been paid. Exasperated by the bureaucratic delays, the Belle-Île paymaster wrote a letter to the *Figaro* newspaper, and its publication caused a minor scandal. Donations mounted up to compensate for the Administration's incompetence.

One of the chambers at Kéréon, with a Hungarian oak floor and box bed.

This could be a good illustration of the "French paradox"—an administration which refuses to pay the heroic Matelot family, while building sumptuous lighthouses (12,500 sheets of opaline, for example, adorn the vast stairwell of Île Vierge!)—but it is of secondary importance. Or perhaps it is the fact that France is one of the world's leading helicopter manufacturers but does not systematically use helicopters, as do the British.[2] But it's not that either. The real paradox of French lighthouses is that, despite a finicky administration, despite methods of financing that pay no heed to the users, despite the civil engineers' architectural flights of fancy and despite centralized Parisian control (leading to the decision to destroy the symbolic Trocadero lighthouse),[3] they do a good job. Their strength lies no doubt in the men, the devotion and the competence of the regional units, and perhaps it's a blessing that there are still 240 keepers, at a time when automation is the rule in other countries.

France is a country fond of records and there is plenty to be proud of: Ar-Men, the lighthouse it took longest to build; Île Vierge, Europe's tallest lighthouse at 75 metres

"You'd have to be stupid not to be afraid in a lighthouse."

(246 feet); and Créac'h, the most powerful European beam. But these exploits are not gratuitous. They are justified by the importance of the English Channel and of the Ouessant shipping lane, the world's busiest maritime zones.

One last structure deserves mention; watching over westernmost France is a building situated to see, rather than to be seen—the opposite of a lighthouse. Built next to the small Ouessant lighthouse, it is similar to an air traffic control tower. Rising 50 metres (164 feet) high, it sways in the wind and is convincing evidence to most visitors that lighthouse-keepers are a brave race indeed. Through the windows can be seen ships passing on the "upstream lane", on their way to Europe from Arabia, South America or Africa, weighed down with petroleum, foodstuffs or iron ore. The tower's radar screens pick them up as little triangles on a brown background, with numbers, similar to the equipment in an airport control tower. Another set of signals on the screens represents south-bound ships on the "downstream lane". Ouessant is the last piece of land they will see until they reach Cape Finisterre, at the tip of the Iberian Peninsula.

(1) There are a few notable exceptions, like Ar-Men and La Jument.
(2) On the other hand, the French pioneered the use of wind pumps.
(3) Officially, this lighthouse has not been destroyed: it was dismantled, but the pieces are nowhere to be found.

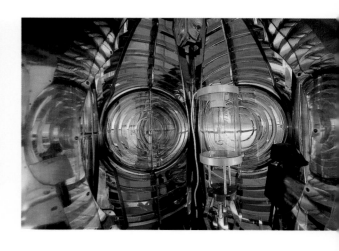

Les Roches Douvres

What will the enormous Roches Douvres buildings be used for after the lighthouse is automated in the year 2000? This was Philippe Camuzard's (bottom) last year as the lighthouse's supervisor. The stairwell (left) looks like a high-rent investment property. To the right of the lighthouse (below) are two windmills, pioneered by the French Lighthouses and Beacons.

Region - Armor coast, entrance to Trieux
Position - 49°06'5"N - 2°48'8"W
Year of construction - 1868, 1954
Engineer - Auffret & Hardion
Height - 60 metres/197 feet
Height above sea level - 65 metres/214 feet
Date of automation - Estimated date 2000
Visibility - 28 miles
Optics - Fresnel
Lights - 1 white flash. 5 seconds
Foghorn - 1 signal. 60 seconds
Helipad - Yes
Open to the public - No
Inhabited - Yes

Region - Armor coast, entrance to Trieux
Position - 48°54'5"N - 3°05'2"W
Year of construction - 1840
Engineer - Léonce Reynaud
Height - 48 metres/157 feet
Height above sea level - 57 metres/187 feet
Date of automation - 1982
Visibility - 15 miles white, 11 miles red, green
Optics - Fresnel
Lights - 3 flashes. 12 seconds
Helipad - No
Open to the public - No
Inhabited - No

Les Héaux de Bréhat

The Héaux de Bréhat marks an area that attracts
many fishermen as the waters abound
in fish. This lighthouse stands 54 metres/177 feet
above the water and is one of the most austere,
but has some elements of a landbased structure.

Region - Armor coast
Position - 48°52'8"N - 3°29'5"W
Year of construction - 1854, 1952
Engineer - Auffret & Hardion
Height - 20 metres/66 feet
Height above sea level - 59 metres/194 feet

Visibility - 24 miles
Optics - Fresnel
Lights - 1 white flash. 15 seconds
Helipad - No
Open to the public - Yes
Inhabited - Yes

Les Sept Îles

The light of Sept Îles viewed from the Ploumanac'h lighthouse (centre). The oldest lighthouse keeper on Sept Îles is Castor the dog, who has been on the mainland only once in 14 years. Bottom right: two keepers and their passions: Gérard Milon (facing the camera) makes ships in bottles, and his colleague, Auguste Carvennec, specializes in growing excellent potatoes!

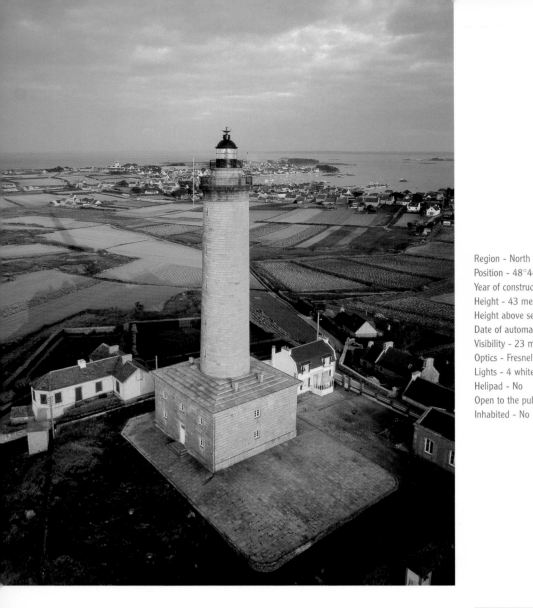

Region - North Finistère
Position - 48°44' 8"N - 4°01'6"W
Year of construction - 1836
Height - 43 metres/141 feet
Height above sea level - 71 metres/233 feet
Date of automation - 1995
Visibility - 23 miles
Optics - Fresnel
Lights - 4 white flashes. 25 seconds
Helipad - No
Open to the public - Yes
Inhabited - No

Île de Batz

The lighthouse on the Île de Batz stands like a monument in the middle of the fields. It is highly visible from the Brittany ferry route from Roscoff to Plymouth. The lighthouse is no longer inhabited, but an association maintains activities during the summer months.

Île Vierge

The lighthouse stairs are lined with 12,500 sheets
of opaline. There are 397 steps.

Île Vierge

The lighthouse on Île Vierge, with its 77-metre/253-foot tower, is the highest in Europe. The three lighthouse keepers, Jean Malgorn, Louis Magueur and Jean Prigent, stand at the window (bottom).

Region - North Finistère
Position - 48°38'4"N - 4°34'1"W
Year of construction - 1845, 1902
Height - 82 metres/269 feet
Height above sea level -
84 metres/276 feet
Visibility - 27 miles
Optics - Fresnel
Lights - 1 white flash. 5 seconds
Foghorn - 1 signal. 60 seconds
Helipad - Yes
Open to the public - Yes
Inhabited - Yes

Île Vierge is a series of low reefs, which are so scattered (centre) that a lighthouse had to be visible from far away; this explains the tower's height.

Le Four illustrates the French paradox
in a spectacular way: this reconstruction
of a medieval tower, built in 1874, is
actually a submarine when the wind blows.
The lighthouse vibrates so much under
the battering of the waves that a table can
be pushed several feet across the room.
It is impossible to land here; crews have to
be winched up and down.

Le Four

Region - North Finistère, Aberwrac'h
Position - 48°31'4"N - 4°48'3"W
Year of construction - 1874
Height - 28 metres/91 feet
Height above sea level - 31 metres/102 feet
Date of automation - 1993
Visibility - 18 miles
Optics - Fresnel
Lights - 5 white flashes. 15 seconds
Foghorn - 5 signals (3 & 2). 60 seconds
Helipad - No
Open to the public - No
Inhabited - No

Region - North Finistère, île d'Ouessant
Position - 48°28'5"N - 5°03'4"W
Year of construction - 1695
Height - 32 metres/105 feet
Height above sea level -
85 metres/279 feet
Date of automation - 1993
Visibility - 24 miles
Optics - Fresnel
Lights - 1 white flash. 20 seconds
Helipad - No
Open to the public - No
Inhabited - No

Le Stiff

The Stiff tower was constructed in 1695; the light was installed where an open fire once stood. This is one of the most stragetic sites on the Atlantic coast: behind Stiff, the Ouessant radar tower monitors the traffic of the 52,000 ships that pass the far western tip of Brittany, at land's end.

The Créac'h lighthouses the Musée officiel des Phares et Balises (Official Museum of Lighthouse and Beacons).

Créac'h

The Créac'h lighthouse is one of the most powerful in the world. It was constructed in 1863, and the panelled and marquetry interior (like the ceiling, left) display an unusual level of luxury. At its base is a museum, which exhibits the most beautiful collection of Fresnel lenses in Europe.

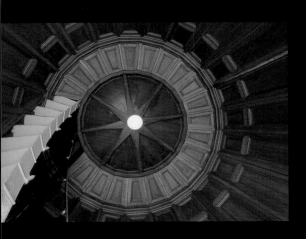

Region - North Finistère, île d'Ouessant
Position - 48°27'6"N - 5°07'8"W
Year of construction - 1863
Engineer - Rousseau
Height - 55 metres/180 feet
Height above sea level - 74 metres/243 feet
Visibility - 32 miles
Optics - Fresnel
Lights - 2 white flashes. 10 seconds
Foghorn - 2 signals. 120 seconds
Helipad - No
Open to the public - Yes (museum)
Inhabited - Yes

Nividic

It took fourteen years to construct
Nividic. The lighthouse can never
be reached, nor can it be inhabited.
Before the helipad was installed,
monitoring crews took a chairlift,
whose pylons were spaced at
900-metre/3,000-feet intervals.
Today, it is powered by solar panels.
Opposite: On 5 January 1998,
the wind reached 180 kph/110 mph
during the aerial shots.

Region - North Finistère, île d'Ouessant
Position - 48°26'8"N - 5°09'1"W
Year of construction - 1936
Height - 28 metres/91 feet
Height above sea level -
36 metres/118 feet
Visibility - 9 miles
Optics - Fresnel
Lights - 9 white flashes. 10 seconds
Helipad - No
Open to the public - No
Inhabited - No

La Jument

The lighthouse at La Jument signals the Fromveur channel, one of Brittany's most dangerous passages. The tower was constructed in record time to take advantage of the Potron bequest (see page 110), but it took 20 more years to strengthen and stabilize it.

Region - North Finistère, île d'Ouessant
Position - 48°25'4"N - 5°08'1"W
Year of construction - 1911
Height - 47 metres/154 feet
Height above sea level - 41 metres/135 feet
Date of automation - 1991
Visibility - 22 miles

Optics - Fresnel
Lights - 3 red flashes. 15 seconds
Foghorn - 3 signals. 60 seconds
Helipad - No
Open to the public - No
Inhabited - No

Like La Jument, Kéréon was financed by a private donor. The luxury of the interior seems almost surrealist in the midst of this wind-battered reef between Ouessant and Molène. Everything had to be unloaded by winches. It took four years of adminstrative procedures to obtain the authorisation and the privilege of visiting this lighthouse for 20 minutes.

Kéréon

Region - North Finistère, île d'Ouessant
Position - 48°26'3"N - 5°01'6"W
Year of construction - 1916
Height - 48 metres/157 feet
Height above sea level - 44 metres/144 feet
Visibility - 19 miles white, 7 miles red
Optics - Fresnel
Lights - 2 flashes. 24 seconds
Foghorn - 3 signals (2 & 1). 120 seconds
Helipad - No
Open to the public - No
Inhabited - Yes

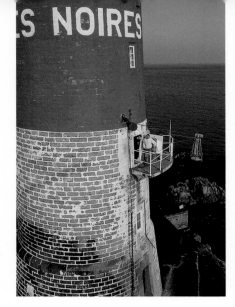

Region - North Finistère, north Iroise
Position - 48°18'7"N - 4°54'9"W
Year of construction - 1872
Height - 28 metres/91 feet
Height above sea level - 30 metres/98 feet
Date of automation - 1992
Visibility - 20 miles
Optics - Fresnel
Lights - 1 red flash. 5 seconds
Foghorn - 2 signals. 60 seconds
Helipad - No
Open to the public - No
Inhabited - No

The lighthouse at Pierres Noires
is now automated. When lighthouse
keepers still lived here, they
were ferried across by a type of
chairlift, which crossed over
the rocks in the foreground (right).
The trip could take up to 10 minutes
in raging seas, which must have
seemed interminably long.

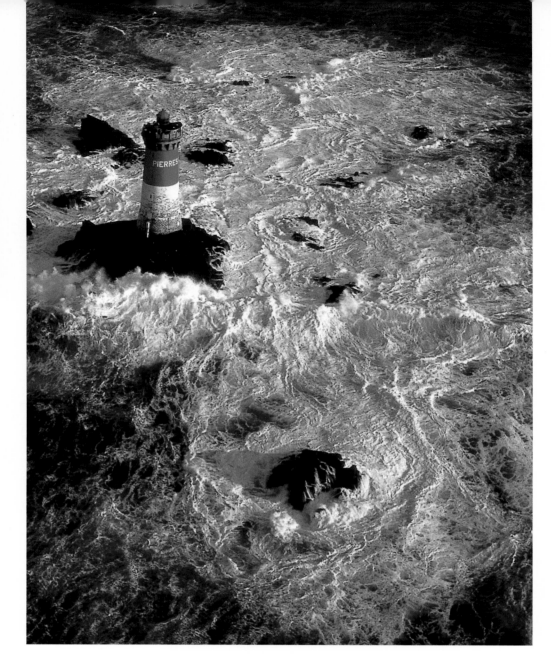

Les Pierres Noires

Saint-Mathieu

Pointe Saint-Mathieu is an amazing site, with the ancient, roofless ruins of an abbey and the red and white shaft of the lighthouse, constructed in 1835. Look at how serene Brittany looks, well-protected by its cliffs and its reefs.

Region - North Finistère, Four channel
Position - 48°19'8"N - 4°46'3"W
Year of construction - 1740, 1821, 1835
Height - 37 metres/121 feet
Height above sea level - 56 metres/184 feet
Visibility - 29 miles
Optics - Fresnel
Lights - 1 white flash. 15 seconds
Helipad - No
Open to the public - Yes
Inhabited - Yes

Ar-Men

The Ar-Men reef was fully submerged, and the currents could reach up to 8 knots (four times the speed of a swimmer). It took 14 years of heroic efforts to build this 29-metre/95-foot tower. Below: the former carbide lamp at Ar-Men (on display at Ouessant). It has been electrified since 1988.

Region - South Finistère, Île de Sein
Position - 48°03'0"N - 4°59'9"W
Year of construction - 1881
Engineer - Léonce Reynaud
Height - 32 metres/105 feet
Height above sea level - 37 metres/121 feet
Date of automation - 1990
Visibility - 23 miles
Optics - Fresnel
Lights - 3 white flashes. 20 seconds
Foghorn - 3 signals. 60 seconds
Helipad - No
Open to the public - No
Inhabited - No

Sein

The Sein lighthouse is not only autonomous, it also produces electricity and drinking water for the storm-battered island. The lighthouse keeper Jean Le Gall (below left) stands next to the lens, which has a visilibity range of 23 miles.

Region - South Finistère, île de Sein
Position - 48°02'6"N - 4°52'1"W
Year of construction - 1838, 1951
Height - 51 metres/168 feet
Height above sea level - 49 metres/161 feet
Visibility - 23 miles
Optics - Fresnel
Lights - 4 white flashes. 25 seconds
Helipad - No
Open to the public - No
Inhabited - Yes

At night, the light of La Vieille (in the foreground to the right) stands in good company: to the left, La Plate; between the two, the Sein lighthouse; and barely visible to its right, the lighthouse of Ar-Men. A ship, just a dot of light, is going up the Raz de Sein. When the lighthouse was automated in 1995, the lighthouse keepers were winched up by helicopter for the first and last time. After 20 years here, the lighthouse supervisor, Jean Donnart, wipes away a tear.

La Vieille

Region - South Finistère, Raz de Sein
Position - 48°02'5"N - 4°45'4"W
Year of construction - 1887
Engineer - Fenoux
Height - 27 metres/88 feet
Height above sea level - 33 metres/108 feet
Date of automation - 1995
Visibility - 19 miles
Optics - Fresnel
Lights - 3 occulting white, red, green. 12 seconds
Foghorn - 3 signals. 60 seconds
Helipad - No
Open to the public - No
Inhabited - No

Eckmühl

The luxurious Eckmühl lighthouse was financed by private donors, in memory of Napoleon's field marshall of the same name (whose statue stands on the ground floor). Taken with a telephoto lens, this photograph illlustrates a line of towers (Eckmühl, with the nearby old lighthouse and the beacons), engulfed by the Atlantic.

Region - South Finistère, Penmarc'h
Position - 47°47'9"N - 4°22'4"W
Year of construction - 1897
Height - 60 metres/197 feet
Height above sea level -
65 metres/214 feet
Visibility - 23 miles

Optics - Fresnel
Lights - 1 white flash. 5 seconds
Foghorn - 1 signal. 60 seconds
Helipad - No
Open to the public - Yes
Inhabited - Yes

Pen-Men

On the Île de Groix,
Jean-Pierre Dizeul performs
the maintenance operations
on his lighthouse with
meticulous care. Some
50 lights around the Morbihan
are managed from here.

Region - Morbihan, île de Groix
Position - 47°38'9"N - 3°30'5"W
Year of construction - 1938
Height - 28 metres/91 feet
Height above sea level -
59 metres/194 feet
Visibility - 29 miles
Optics - Fresnel
Lights - 4 white flashes. 25 seconds
Helipad - No
Open to the public - No
Inhabited - Yes

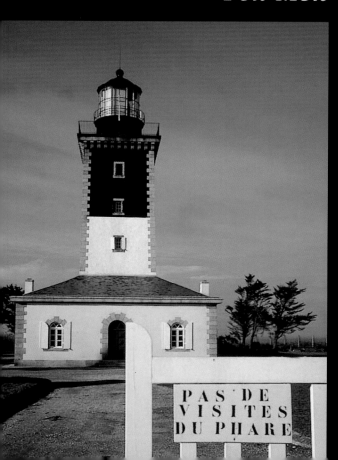

PAS DE
VISITES
DU PHARE

136

On 26 November 1996, a storm struck Belle-Île: this is certainly the most widely distributed image of any lighthouse in the world (more than 400,000 copies to date). The first lens installed at Les Poulains (below left) is exhibited at the Goulphar Museum.

Les Poulains

Region - Morbihan, Belle-Île
Position - 47°23'3"N - 3°15'1"W
Year of construction - 1899
Height - 15 metres/49 feet
Height above sea level - 34 metres/111 feet
Date of automation - 1987
Visibility - 23 miles
Optics - Fresnel
Lights - 1 white flash. 5 seconds
Helipad - No
Open to the public - No
Inhabited - No

PHARE
DE
GOULPHAR

Goulphar houses a small museum about the island's lighthouses.

Goulphar

If you were looking for an archetypical Republican monument, it would be Goulphar, which is as solemn as a lay church and duly illuminated at night. The three keepers are Michel Granger, the supervisor, Yves Gueho and René Leport (bottom), a former keeper at Ar-Men.

Region - Morbihan, Belle-Île
Position - 47°18'7"N - 3°13'6"W
Year of construction - 1836
Engineer - Léonor Fresnel
Height - 52 metres/171 feet
Height above sea level - 87 metres/285 feet
Visibility - 26 miles
Optics - Fresnel
Lights - 2 white flashes. 10 seconds
Helipad - No
Open to the public - Yes
Inhabited - Yes

Le Pilier

The Pilier lighthouse is a dual structure. The old lighthouse, too narrow to house a powerful light, stands in the foreground. The current tower, the square building just behind the first, was built in 1877. In the background is an old bastion; before it became a danger to navigation, the Pilier was a fortress defending the Vendée region.

Region - Vendée
Position - 47°02'60"N - 02°21'60"W
Year of construction - 1877 - 1829 - 1876
Engineer - Dingler
Height - 34 metres/111 feet
Height above sea level - 33 metres/108 feet
Date of automation - 1996
Visibility - 29 miles
Optics - Fresnel
Lights - 3 white flashes. 20 seconds
Helipad - No
Open to the public - No
Inhabited - No

The 34-metre/111-foot Petite Foule tower is the only large Art Deco lighthouse in France (even though this style was already out of fashion in 1950). It is a highly successful design, and it's a shame that the living quarters are not well maintained.

Petite Foule

Region - Vendée, île d'Yeu
Position - 46°43'10"N - 02°22'90"W
Year of construction - 1829-1831
Engineer - Duran
Height - 38 metres/125 feet
Height above sea level - 56 metres/184 feet
Date of automation - 1980
Visibility - 24 miles
Optics - Fresnel
Lights - 1 white flash. 5 seconds
Helipad - No
Open to the public - Yes
Inhabited - Yes

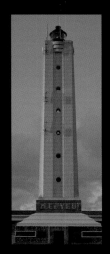

The Baleines lighthouse on Île de Ré was constructed in 1854, but another smaller light already existed (in the background). The Baleines lens is, like the one at Goulphar, highly complex. Before coming here, Georges Sadou had been a keeper at Triagoz for 17 years.

Les Baleines

Region - Charente Maritime, Île de Ré
Position - 46°14'70''N - 01°33'70''W
Year of construction - 1699, 1854
Engineer - LeGros
Height - 53 metres/175 feet
Height above sea level -
57 metres/187 feet
Visibility - 24 miles
Optics - Fresnel
Lights - 4 white flashes. 15 seconds
Helipad - No
Open to the public - Yes
Inhabited - Yes

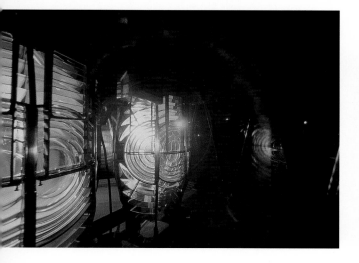

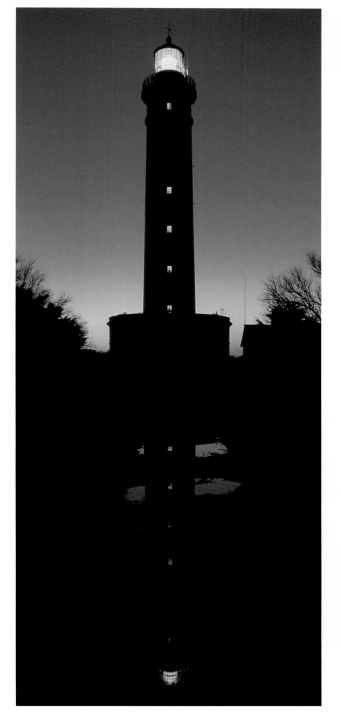

Chassiron

Constructed in 1836, the Chassiron tower is a beautifully austere structure. The lighthouse is now automated. Although the living quarters are in very poor condition, Chassiron is, with the Baleines lighthouse, one of the most highly visited lighthouses in France.

Region - Charente Maritime, Île d'Oléron	Visibility - 28 miles
Position - 46°02'9"N - 01°24'5"W	Optics - Fresnel
Year of construction - 1836	Lights - 1 white flash. 10 seconds
Engineer - Leclerc	Helipad - No
Height - 46 metres/151 feet	Open to the public - Yes
Height above sea level - 50 metres/165 feet	Inhabited - No

La Coubre

When the Coubre lighthouse was
constructed in 1905, it stood
1.5 kilometres (1 mile) from the sea,
but the pounding waves have cut
that distance down to 250 metres
(820 feet). The barbette on the side
of the tower houses a second light.
The man closing the curtains (right),
to protect the lens from the sun,
is Michel Thomas, who spent 14
years at the Four lighthouse.

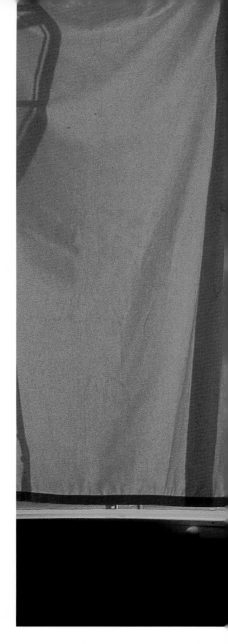

Region - Charente Maritime
Position - 45°41'8"N - 01°14'00"W
Year of construction - 1860, 1895, 1905
Height - 64 metres/210 feet
Height above sea level - 65 metres/213 feet
Visibility - 28 miles
Optics - Fresnel
Lights - 2 white flashes. 10 seconds
Helipad - No
Open to the public - Yes
Inhabited - Yes

Cordouan, an obelisk guarding the entrance to the Gironde, is both sublime and miraculous: sublime for its well-proportioned design and classical forms; miraculous because the overall effect is so successful. Indeed, the current tower was created in 1789, when a lighthouse was placed on the third floor of a Baroque monument constructed in 1611. Begun in 1584 by Louis de Foix, Cordouan symbolized the king and the church, which explains the royal apartments and a chapel. Dominique Pardoux is one of the lighthouse keepers who watch over the structure, but the luxurious interior is deteriorating.

"Louis XIV, roi très chrétien, a remis en état depuis ses fondations, cette tour de Cordouan qui gouvernait, par ses feux nocturnes, la course des bateaux à travers l'embouchure peu profonde de la Garonne. An 1665.

Louis XV a consolidé par de nouveaux travaux et a ordonné que soit placé au-dessus un phare de fer plus haut et plus important à la place de l'ancien en pierre. An 1727."

Text over the entrance to the chapel.

Cordouan

A central well cuts through the chapel at Cordouan (left), as well as through all the other floors right to the top. The red and green sectors are clearly visible in the lantern, in which stand two of the keepers, Loïc Couriaut and Serge Andron (the latter is a specialist in making boats in bottles). The crew is changed at mid-tide; they reach the lighthouse from Peyrat, constructed in 1720 on a sandbank.

Region - Gironde
Position - 45°35'2"N - 1°10'4"W
Year of construction - 1584
Engineer - Louis de Foix
Height - 60 metres/197 feet
Height above sea level - 68 metres/223 feet
Date of automation - 1990
Visibility - 22 miles
Optics - Fresnel
Lights - White, red, green: 3 occ. 12 seconds
Helipad - No
Open to the public - Yes
Inhabited - Yes

Cap Ferret

The lighthouse at Cap Ferret, which marks the entrance to the Bassin d'Arcachon, is a metal structure. Dominique Tobie, now retired, was the last keeper at the lighthouse: the 360° light is now automated.

Region - Gironde
Position - 44°38'7"N - 01°15'00"W
Year of construction - 1840, 1948
Height - 52 metres/171 feet
Height above sea level - 53 metres/174 feet
Date of automation - 1995
Visibility - 27 miles
Optics - Fresnel
Lights - 1 red flash. 5 seconds
Helipad - No
Open to the public - Yes
Inhabited - No

Contis

A distinctive lighthouse had to be built to stand out against the uniform landscape of the Landes coast. This is why a spiral was painted along its entire length. Now the lighthouse has been automated, the living quarters are used as holiday homes for civil servants.

Region - Landes forest
Position - 44°05'70''N - 01°19'20''W
Year of construction - 1863
Height - 42 metres/138 feet
Height above sea level -
50 metres/165 feet
Date of automation - 1999

Visibility - 23 miles
Optics - Fresnel
Lights - 4 white flashes. 25 seconds
Helipad - No
Open to the public - Yes
Inhabited - Yes

Pointe Saint-Martin

At Biarritz, the city of lights,
the lighthouse seems to
be yet another attraction
intended for the tourists.
The simplicity and elegance
of this lighthouse can be
explained by its date of
construction, 1830, before
the decision was taken to
make all French lighthouses
resemble fortresses.

Region - Pyrénées Atlantiques, Biarritz
Position - 43°29'6"N - 01°33'3"W
Year of construction - 1834
Engineer - Vionnois
Height - 47 metres/154 feet
Height above sea level - 73 metres/240 feet
Date of automation - 1980

Visibility - 29 miles
Optics - Fresnel
Lights - 2 white flashes. 10 seconds
Helipad - No
Open to the public - Yes
Inhabited - No

La Croix

Region - Armor coast, entrance to Trieux
Position - 48°50'3"N - 3°3'3"W
Year of construction - 1865, 1949
Height - 15 metres/49 feet
Height above sea level -
23 metres/75 feet

Visibility - 19 miles
Optics - Fresnel
Lights - White: 1 occ. 4 second
Helipad - No
Open to the public - No
Inhabited - No

La Croix (left) was destroyed in 1940-45, but an identical structure was rebuilt. The roof at Triagoz collapsed amid total indifference. Yet look at the diversity of these lighthouses...

Les Triagoz

Region - Armor coast, Lézardrieux
Position - 48°52'3"N - 3°38'8"W
Year of construction - 1864
Engineer - Pelaud
Height - 30 metres/98 feet
Height above sea level -
31 metres/102 feet
Date of automation - 1984

Visibility - 14 miles white, 11 m
Optics - Fresnel
Lights - White and red:
2 occultations. 6 seconds
Helipad - No
Open to the public - No
Inhabited - No

La Lande

Region - Morlaix River
Position - 48°38'2"N - 3°53'1"W
Year of construction - 1845
Height -19 metres/62 feet
Height above sea level -
87 metres/285 feet
Date of automation - 1993

Visibility - 23 miles
Optics - Fresnel
Lights - 1 white flash. 5 second
Helipad - No
Open to the public - No
Inhabited - Yes

Pointe du Petit Minou

Region - Finistère, Brest channel
Position - 48°20'2"N - 4°36'9"W
Year of construction - 1848
Height - 26 metres/85 feet
Height above sea level -
32 metres/105 feet
Date of automation - 1989

Visibility - 19 miles white, 15 mi
Optics - Fresnel
Lights - 2 flashes. 6 seconds
Foghorn - 1 signal. 60 seconds
Helipad - No
Open to the public - No
Inhabited - No

Portzic

Region - Finistère, Brest channel
Position - 48°21'6"N - 4°32'0"W
Year of construction - 1848
Height - 35 metres/115 feet
Height above sea level -
58 metres/190 feet
Date of automation - 1995

Visibility - 19 miles white,
15 miles red
Optics - Fresnel
Lights - 2 flashes. 12 seconds
Helipad - No
Open to the public - No
Inhabited - Yes

Lighthouses have become an
essential part of our coastlines.
No one questions whether they are
beautiful or ugly; they are there, and
we strongly hope they will remain!

Île aux Moutons

Region - South Finistère
Position - 47°46'5"N - 4°01'7"W
Year of construction - 1878
Height - 17 metres/56 feet
Height above sea level -
20 metres/66 feet
Date of automation - 1983

Visibility - 15 miles
Optics - Fresnel
Lights - White, red, green:
2 occultations. 6 seconds
Helipad - No
Open to the public - No
Inhabited - No

Penfret

Region - Finistère, Glénan Islands
Position - 47°43'30"N - 03°57'20"W
Year of construction - 1838
Height - 24 metres/79 feet
Height above sea level -
38 metres/125 feet
Date of automation - 1993

Visibility - 21 miles
Optics - Fresnel
Lights - 1 red flash. 5 seconds
Helipad - No
Open to the public - No
Inhabited - No

Pointe des Chats

Region - Morbihan, Île de Groix
Position - 47°37'3"N - 3°25'3"W
Year of construction - 1907
Height - 15 metres/49 feet
Height above sea level -
16 metres/52 feet

Visibility - 29 miles
Optics - Fresnel
Lights - 1 red flash. 5 seconds
Helipad - No
Open to the public - No
Inhabited - Yes

Tevennec

Region - South Finistère, Raz de Sein
Position - 48°04'3"N - 4°47'6"W
Year of construction - 1875
Height - 15 metres/49 feet
Height above sea level -
28 metres/91 feet
Date of automation - 1910

Visibility - 9 miles white, 6 miles re
Optics - Fresnel
Lights - Flashing white and red
Helipad - No
Open to the public - No
Inhabited - No

The purpose of a lighthouse is to be in the wildest and most dangerous places. The *Norway* (the former *France*) passing by adds to the spectacle.

La Teignouse

Region - Morbihan
Position - 47°27'5"N - 3°02'8"W
Year of construction - 1845
Height - 16 metres/52 feet
Height above sea level -
20 metres/66 feet
Date of automation - 1983

Visibility - 15 miles
Optics - Fresnel
Lights -white and red flash. 4 seconds
Helipad - No
Open to the public - No
Inhabited - No

Penlan

Region - Morbihan, entrance to Vilaine
Position - 47°31'0"N - 2°30'2"W
Year of construction - 1881
Height - 16 metres/52 feet
Height above sea level -
26 metres/85 feet
Date of automation - 1995

Visibility - 15 miles white,
11 miles red and green
Optics - Fresnel
Lights - 2 occultations. 6 seconds
Helipad - No
Open to the public - No
Inhabited - Yes

Plateau du Four

Region - Loire Atlantique,
Plateau du Four
Position - 47°17'9"N - 2°38'1"W
Year of construction -1822, 1846
Height - 23 metres/75 feet
Height above sea level -
27 metres/88 feet

Date of automation - 1984
Visibility - 18 miles
Optics - Fresnel
Lights - 1 white flash. 5 seconds
Helipad - No
Open to the public - No
Inhabited - No

La Banche

Region - Loire Atlantique
Position - 47°10'6"N - 02°28'1"W
Year of construction - 1865
Engineer - Mr. Paul Leferme
Height - 22 metres/72 feet
Height above sea level -
30 metres/98 feet
Date of automation - 1986

Visibility - 18 miles
Optics - Fresnel
Lights - 3 white and red flashes.
15 seconds
Helipad - No
Open to the public - No
Inhabited - No

Le Grand Charpentier

Region - Loire Atlantique
Position - 47°12'51"N - 2°19'19"W
Year of construction - 1888
Height - 22 metres/72 feet
Height above sea level -
27 metres/88 feet
Date of automation - 1972
Visibility - 14 miles white
10 miles red and green

Optics - Fresnel
Lights - Flashing white, red and
green
Helipad - No
Open to the public - No
Inhabited - No

Square or slender, rising up from
meadows or solid rocks, dull or
brightly colored, lighthouses mark
the coastal landscape as do belltowers
on the mainland.

Pointe des Corbeaux

Region - Loire Atlantique, île d'Yeu
Position - 41°41'4"N - 2°17'1"W
Year of construction - 1868 - 1950
Engineer - Duran
Height - 19 metres/62 feet
Height above sea level -
25 metres/82 feet

Date of automation - 1979
Visibility - 20 miles
Optics - Fresnel
Lights - 3 red flashes. 15 seconds
Helipad - No
Open to the public - No
Inhabited - No

Hourtin

Region - Gironde, Hourtin Lake
Position - 45°08'50"N - 01°09'70"W
Year of construction - 1863
Height - 24 metres/79 feet
Height above sea level -
55 metres/180 feet
Date of automation - 1980

Visibility - 23 miles
Optics - Fresnel
Lights - 1 white flash. 5 seconds
Helipad - No
Open to the public - No
Inhabited - No

Socoa

Region - Pyrénées Atlantiques,
Saint-Jean-de-Luz
Position - 43°23'80"N - 01°41'10"W
Year of construction - 1844
Height - 12 metres/39 feet
Height above sea level -
36 metres/118 feet
Date of automation - Early 1970s

Visibility - 12 miles white,
8 miles red
Optics - Fresnel
Lights - Flashing white and red
Helipad - No
Open to the public - No
Inhabited - Yes

The Iberian Lighthouses

Northern Spain: a Surprising Concentration of Lighthouses

The North Sea separates the Shetlands from the Orkneys, and the Pentland Firth cuts off the Orkneys from Scotland. St George's Channel keeps Ireland away from Wales, and the English Channel holds England at a distance from France. France, however, is separated from Spain by the mere 30 metres (98 feet) of the Bidassoa River, which lies some 1,600 kilometres (1,000 miles) as the crow flies to the south of the Shetland Islands.

Although this looks like it may be the end of the Atlantic coastline, it still runs another 1,600 kilometres (1,000 miles) from Irun to Gibraltar. Spain is generally considered to be a Mediterranean country, but a look at an atlas offers a different picture. The Costa Verde, which includes the Basque and Asturian coasts, is as long as Ireland, and Galicia is the size of Brittany. Portugal is as elongated as England.

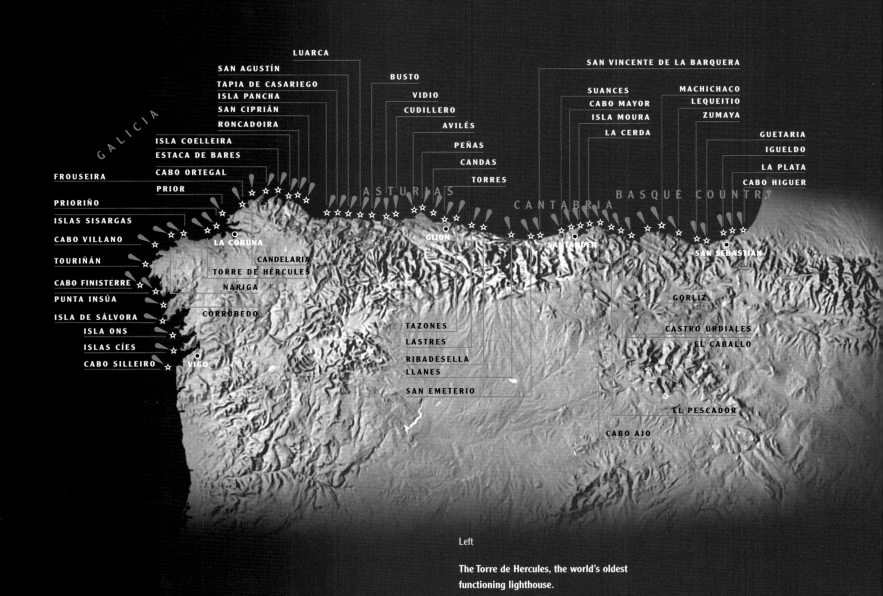

Left

The Torre de Hercules, the world's oldest functioning lighthouse.

This long coastline is not the only surprising thing about the Iberian Peninsula. The Costa Verde is, in fact, the industrial heart of Spain. Bilbao is the equivalent of Le Havre, Gijón of Dunkerque, and El Ferrol of Brest. Three of Spain's leading six commercial ports are here, including the largest (Bilbao). And even the tourist city of San Sebastián, summer residence of Alfonso XIII, hides an industrial port. A few kilometres to the east, there is a fault in the cliff, and ships can just get through the Pasajes passage, which suddenly opens out into a vast bay, bordered with quays and cranes, canning factories, expressways and rundown buildings. Farther west along the coast, factories suddenly appear amid the mountainous scenery. In the middle of a delightfully rural setting is a huge refinery. Farther still along this same spectacular road, which runs between sea and mountain, is a mining cableway.

Machichaco

Despite the factories, the landscape is breathtaking. Torrents cascade down mountaintops, hollowing out valleys, forming the many rivers that reach the coastline—one about every 15 kilometres (9 miles).

The Atlantic shoreline of the Iberian Peninsula boasts forty-two major lighthouses (a "major lighthouse" is defined as one with visibility of at least 20 nautical miles); this is more than Scotland, Ireland or France. But you won't find an Ar-Men, an Eddystone or a Skerryvore here. There are no rock lighthouses, none of the granite towers built from blood, sweat and tears. There are no rock lighthouses, simply because there are no isolated reefs. According to navigational charts, "the [Cantabrian] coast is rocky, uneven and bordered with many steep slopes. It is generally safe ... The 20-metre (65-foot) isobath is usually less than 0.5 metres (1 1/2 feet) from the shore."

In other words, the imaginary line that connects points of an underwater depth of 20 metres runs less than 900 metres (3,000 feet) from the coast, sometimes much less. The first Asturian lighthouse, San Emeterio, stands on top of a 60-metre (197-foot) cliff, and the water is so deep that ships can sail close to it.

Without isolated reefs to beacon, the Iberian lighthouses serve two purposes. First, they signal the capes: Cabo Machichaco, Mayor, Torres, Estaca de Bares, Ortegal, Fisterra, and, farther on, the tip of the Berlenga Islands, Cabo da Roca, São Vicente then Gibraltar. Second, they indicate the ports.

The first lighthouses after France, Cabo Higuer, San Sebastián, Machichaco and so on set the tone for what comes next. The British may have invented the rock-lighthouse, but the Spanish created the house-lighthouse. The concept is simple: they started with a spectacular site, perched high somewhere along the coast, planted a house there and made it a cross between an estancia and a hunting-lodge. They then added a low, ornate tower, known by architects as a "folly", crowned it with a lantern and placed plenty of glasswork in the domed roof. There are variations on the theme: Machichaco is as solemn as a palace, Lequeitio looks like an isolated chapel and Llanes resembles a detached suburban house. There are also exceptions: Cabo Villano is a solid two-storey building next to a peak on top of which is a pretty hexagonal tower; the tower is linked to the main building via a tunnel built over the rock. Frouseira (built in 1970 and automated from the start) is a solitary parallelepiped, a Bauhaus version of a lighthouse. And then there is the Torre de Hércules. This edifice is unclassifiable, having been modified many times since it was erected by Caius

Cabo Villano

Sevius Lupus under the Roman emperor Trajan. The Torre de Hercules is the world's oldest working lighthouse; its stonework encompasses nineteen centuries of history. The tower, which has been remodelled four times, is, at 54 metres (177 feet) also one of the tallest on the peninsula.

The Torre de Hércules signals the odd town of La Coruña, which is so cramped on a peninsula that its "sea" side and "bay" side are only 200 metres (650 feet) apart. On this north-western tip of Spain, it is difficult to distinguish "capes" and "bays", because the coast is so jagged and indented: it consists of a mixture of *rias* and rocks, clustered around Cabo Fisterra. The famous cape has a charmless lighthouse–which is of no importance, because passing ships cannot see it at all. This is because the shipping lane is 30 miles out to sea; ships going upstream, and a little farther out those going downstream, sail along in single file (as they do off Ouessant). The second reason is precipitation: at Pontevedra, just to the south, it rains every other day for nine months a year, and the south-westerly wind can whip up a dense fog in minutes. We were nearing the Sisargas islands (between La Coruña and Fisterra) when the horizon suddenly disappeared behind a real pea-souper; we kept on, guided by the lighthouse foghorn. We had nearly arrived and were expecting to see the lighthouse at any minute, when someone suddenly looked up and spotted

The Torre de Hercules is the world's oldest working lighthouse; its stonework encompasses nineteen centuries of history.

the lighthouse almost on top of us, 100 metres (330 feet) above on a cliff. As we sailed round it, we caught sight of the rocks, near enough to reach out and touch. On another occasion, as we were entering the Ria d'Arosa, the superb scenery disappeared in fog in a matter of minutes.

For nearly seventy years, navigators had another reason to fear this spot, as there was one lighthouse too many. The lighthouse of Cabo Corrubedo could be mistaken for the one on Sálvora Island; sailors rounded the first, thinking they had actually rounded the second. In 1896, the *Sarlier* was wrecked on the rocks (280 dead). Fourteen years later, the *Palermo* suffered the same fate (24 victims), but it was not until 1921 that the signals from these lighthouses (built in 1852-54) were clearly differentiated.

The port of Vigo is in the last Galician ria. An octagonal red and white tower, next to what looks like a small barracks, watches over its southern entrance. This lighthouse, Cabo Silleiro, overlooks the port of Baïona, where they play strange local bagpipes, a remnant of the area's Celtic links.

The Torre de Hércules.

Silleiro, the last Galician lighthouse before Portugal.

The lighthouse keeper Manuel Expósito Alvarez
inside the Fresnel lens at the Silleiro lighthouse.

La Plata

Region - Basque country, Pasajes
Position - 43°20'01"N - 1°56'0"W
Year of construction - 1855
Architect - Lafarga
Height - 5 metres/16 feet
Height above sea level - 153 metres/502 feet

Visibility - 13 miles
Optics - Fresnel
Lights - White, occulting 4 seconds
Helipad - No
Open to the public - No
Inhabited - Yes

The Pasajes marks the entrance to an odd commercial port hidden behind a passage as narrow as a river. The dome-shaped lantern is a typical feature of Spanish lighthouses.

Igueldo dominates the western edge of the Bay of San Sebastián. In the middle of the bay is an island with a low-powered lamp. The light-colored tower above the city is not a lighthouse; it is a religious sculpture. Above the lighthouse stands a hotel and a theme park, where the roller coasters plunge straight down toward Igueldo—

Igueldo

guaranteed to frighten!

Region - Basque country, San Sebastián
Position - 43°19'4"N - 2°00'6"W
Year of construction - 1855
Architect - Manuel Peironcely
Height - 13 metres/43 feet
Height above sea level -
134 metres/440 feet
Visibility - 26 miles
Optics - Fresnel
Lights - 3 white flashes (1 + 2). 15 seconds
Helipad - No
Open to the public - No
Inhabited - Yes

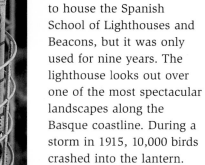

Machichaco

The building at the base of the tower was constructed to house the Spanish School of Lighthouses and Beacons, but it was only used for nine years. The lighthouse looks out over one of the most spectacular landscapes along the Basque coastline. During a storm in 1915, 10,000 birds crashed into the lantern. The lighthouse keeper Alejandro Martínez (left) gives an idea of its size.

Region - Basque country
Position - 43°27'2"N - 2°45'2"W
Year of construction - 1852, 1909
Architect - Rafael de la Cerda
Height - 20 metres/66 feet
Height above sea level -
122 metres/400 feet
Visibility - 24 miles
Optics - Fresnel
Lights - 1 white flash. 7 seconds
Foghorn - Siren signaling the letter M.
60 seconds
Helipad - No
Open to the public - No
Inhabited - Yes

Gorliz

Does a true "Madrid School" of lighthouse architects exist?
In any case, the designers of the most recent Spanish lighthouses are all graduates of the same school in the Spanish capital. The Cabo Villano tower, designed by Enrique Martínez Tercero is extremely elegant. The foundations visible in the foreground did not support lighthouses, but were for cannons placed there to defend the coastline.

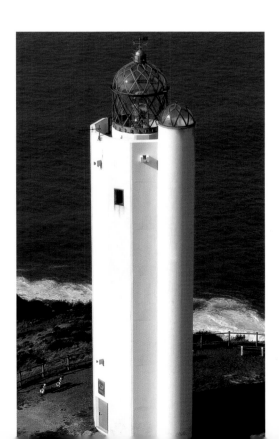

Region - Basque country
Position - 43°26'0"N - 2°56'6"W
Year of construction - 1962, 1989
Architect - Enrique Martínez Tercero
Height - 21 metres/69 feet
Height above sea level -
166 metres/545 feet
Visibility - 22 miles
Optics - Fresnel
Lights - 3 white flashes (1+2). 16 seconds
Helipad - No
Open to the public - No
Inhabited - No

Castro Urdiales

Some purists would like to remove the Castro Urdiales lighthouse, added to a much older chateau-church complex in 1853. But it won't happen! The lighthouse is yet another element in the extraordinary tangle that makes this site so unique. During storms, everything disappears in the mist.

Region - Cantabria
Position - 43°23'1"N - 3°12' 9"W
Year of construction - 1853
Height - 20 metres/66 feet
Height above sea level - 49 metres/161 feet
Visibility - 20 miles
Optics - Revolving light with reflectors
Lights - 4 white flashes. 24 seconds
Foghorn - Siren signalling the letter C. 60 seconds
Helipad - No
Open to the public - No
Inhabited - No

169

The lighthouse of El Pescador, constructed in 1864, originally operated with olive oil, as did all the Spanish lighthouses during this period. The storm in 1915 destroyed a building that stood 15 metres (49 feet) high! From the sea, the whitewashed walls are as visible as the tower itself.

El Pescador

Region - Cantabria
Position - 43°27'9"N - 3°26'1"W
Year of construction - 1864
Height - 13 metres/43 feet
Height above sea level -
39 metres/128 feet
Visibility - 9 miles
Optics - Fresnel
Lights - 4 white flashes (3+1). 15 seconds
Helipad - No
Open to the public - No
Inhabited - No

El Caballo

It takes an eagle to reach an eagle's nest—or else, as at Punta del Caballo, a tough climb up 682 steps carved out of the sheer rock. It's a dream for hikers, but was a nightmare for lighthouse keepers of old.

The Cabo Mayor lighthouse has become the emblem of the city of Santander: it is one of the only Spanish lighthouses open to the public. The view is spectacular today, but the site has a bloody history: dozens of partisans were thrown from the top of this sheer cliff during the Spanish Civil War.

Cabo Mayor

Region - Cantabria
Position - 43°29'5"N - 3°47'4"W
Year of construction - 1839
Engineer - Rogi
Height - 30 metres/98 feet
Height above sea level -
91 metres/299 feet
Visibility - 21 miles

Optics - Fresnel
Lights - 2 white flashes. 10 seconds
Foghorn - Siren signalling the letter
M. 40 seconds
Helipad - No
Open to the public - No
Inhabited - Yes

Torres

Cabo Torres marks the entrance to Gijón, Spain's second-largest commercial port. The living quarters, no longer used, have been adopted by the seagulls, who bombard those adventurous enough to climb up this steep promontory.

Region - Asturias
Position - 43°34'18"N - 5°41'58"W
Year of construction - 1924
Engineer - Jesús Goicoechea
Height - 16 metres/52 feet
Height above sea level -
86 metres/282 feet
Visibility - 25 miles
Optics - Fresnel
Lights - 2 white flashes. 10 seconds
Helipad - No
Open to the public - No
Inhabited - No

172

Peñas

With a visibility of 35 nautical miles (65 km), Peñas is the most powerful lighthouse in Spain. The optics (pictured behind the lighthouse keeper, José Luis García Gómez) were made in France. Yet the equiment is starting to show its age: of the eight original foghorns, only one is still operational.

Region - Asturias
Position - 43°39'3"N - 5°59' 9"W
Year of construction - 1852, 1929
Engineer - Jesús Goicoechea
Height - 19 metres/62 feet
Height above sea level - 119 metres/390 feet
Visibility - 35 miles

Optics - Fresnel
Lights - 3 white flashes. 15 seconds
Foghorn - Siren signalling the letter P. 60 seconds
Helipad - No
Open to the public - No
Inhabited - Yes

Vidio

The Asturian coast is no less rugged than that of the Bay of Biscay, with numerous headlands, estuaries and small ports. The rocky spur of Cabo Vidio, with its lighthouse (constructed in 1950) is even more spectacular than the others.

Region - Asturias
Position - 43°35'36"N - 6°19'42"W
Year of construction - 1950
Engineer - José María González del Valle
Height - 9 metres/30 feet
Height above sea level - 89 metres/292 feet
Visibility - 25 miles

Optics - Fresnel
Lights - 1 flash. 5 seconds
Foghorn - Siren signalling the letter V
Helipad - No
Open to the public - No
Inhabited - Yes

Luarca

Luarca has always been a refuge for fishermen. When the ancient lighthouse was abandoned, the church became their landmark—until 1862, when the current lighthouse was constructed.

Region - Asturias
Position - 43°33'58"N – 6°31' 56"W
Year of construction - 1862
Engineer - Javier Sanz
Height - 10 metres/33 feet
Height above sea level - 53 metres/174 feet
Visibility - 20 miles
Optics - Fresnel
Lights - 3 flashes. 8 seconds
Foghorn - Siren signalling the letter L.
30 seconds
Helipad - No
Open to the public - No
Inhabited - Yes

San Agustín

This lighthouse was constructed after the Second World War, to replace the beacon and the bell, which were not visible or audible enough. It marks the mouth of the Navia River, the largest in the Spanish Pyrenees.

Région - Asturias
Position - 43°33'8"N - 6°44'1"W
Year of construction - 1945, 1975
Engineer - Angel Fernández
Height - 20 meters / 66 feet
Height above sea level - 82 m. / 269 f.

Visibility - 20 miles
Optics - Fresnel
Lights - 2 flashes. 12 seconds
Helipad - No
Open to the public - No
Inhabited - No

Isla Pancha

Fifteen kilometres (9 miles) to
the west of the Navia estuary,
the Eo River created a ria (an inlet),
and the Eo ria became the port of
Ribadeo, whose entrance is signalled
by a recent lighthouse (1984).
It replaces the old 1860 lighthouse on
Isla Pancha, no longer used.

Region - Galicia
Position - 43°33'4"N - 7°02'5"W
Year of construction - 1860, 1984
Height - 13 metres/43 feet
Height above sea level - 28 metres/91 feet
Visibility - 21 miles
Optics - Revolving light with reflectors
Lights - 4 white flashes (3 and 1). 20 seconds
Foghorn - Siren signalling the letter R. 30 seconds
Helipad - No
Open to the public - No
Inhabited - No

Estaca de Bares

Estaca de Bares is the
northernmost point on
the Iberian peninsula.
The wind is strong enough
to rip off doors and
windows if one of them
is left open inadvertently.
The lighthouse keeper,
Mercedes Aranceta,
lives surrounded by her
animals in the spot at
the end of the world.

Region - Galicia
Position - 43°47'2"N - 7°41'1"W
Year of construction - 1849
Engineer - Félix Uhagón
Height - 10.50 metres/34 feet
Height above sea level - 101 metres/331 feet
Visibility - 25 miles
Optics - Fresnel
Lights - 2 white flashes. 7.5 seconds
Foghorn - Siren signalling the letter B.
60 seconds
Helipad - No
Open to the public - No
Inhabited - Yes

The tower at Cabo Ortegal is only 10 metres (33 feet) high, but the lantern dominates the coast at 124 metres (407 feet) above sea level. It is a recent, automated light (1984). Behind these rocks lies Coruña Bay.

Cabo Ortegal

Region - Galicia
Position - 43°46'3"N - 7°52'2"W
Year of construction - 1984
Architect - Jaime Arrandiaga
Height - 10 metres/33 feet
Height above sea level - 124 metres/407 feet

Visibility - 18 miles
Optics - Fresnel
Lights - White, 1 occultation. 8 seconds
Helipad - No
Open to the public - No
Inhabited - No

Torre de Herculés

La Coruña is an odd town, with one side facing the sea and
the other facing the bay (and with just 200 metres/650 feet
of tiny streets between them). At the far northern tip of this peninsula
is the Torre de Hércules, the oldest lighthouse in the world.

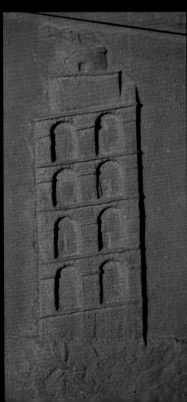

Torre de Herculés

This Roman tower once had a glowing fire at the top. Its current appearance dates from 1847, when 48.5 metres (160 feet) were added by constructing this complex stone turret. A bronze bas-relief (bottom left) illustrates the various transformations the structure has undergone over the centuries. Although a popular tourist site, this monument is nevertheless a navigation aid, manned by lighthouse keeper Emilio González Domínguez.

Region - Galicia
Position - 43°23'2"N - 8°24'3"W
Year of construction - 2nd century AD, 1847
Height - 48.50 metres/159 feet
Height above sea level - 106 metres/348 feet
Visibility - 23 miles
Optics - Fresnel
Lights - 4 white flashes. 20 seconds
Foghorn - Siren signalling the letter L. 30 seconds
Helipad - No
Open to the public - Yes
Inhabited - Yes

Islas Sisargas

Fog can cover the Islas Sisargas
in just a few minutes, and
the light is certainly less effective
than the foghorn, which spells
the letter "S" in Morse code every
30 seconds.

Region - Galicia
Position - 43°21'6"N - 8°50'7"W
Year of construction - 1853
Architect - Celedonio de Uribe
Height - 11 metres/36 feet
Height above sea level - 110 metres/361 feet
Visibility - 23 miles
Optics - Fresnel
Lights - 3 white flashes. 15 seconds
Foghorn - Siren signalling the letter S. 30 seconds
Helipad - No
Open to the public - No
Inhabited - Yes

Nariga

The Nariga lighthouse is brand new: 1998. Jesús Martínez Román, known as "Sito", is the keeper at Nariga, but he also takes care of Sisargas and is a philosophy student. He feels that the lighthouse is the only place where he can study in peace and quiet.

Region - Galicia
Position - 43°19'3"N - 8°54'5"W
Year of construction - 1998
Architect - César Portela
Height - 30 metres/98 feet
Height above sea level -
55 metres/180 feet
Visibility - 22 miles
Optics - Fresnel
Lights - 4 white flashes (3+1). 20 seconds
Helipad - No
Open to the public - No
Inhabited - No

Region - Galicia
Position - 43°09'6"N - 9°12'7"W
Year of construction - 1896
Engineer - Salvador López Miño
Height - 24 metres/79 feet
Height above sea level - 104 metres/341 feet
Visibility - 27 miles
Optics - Fresnel
Lights - 2 white flashes. 15 seconds
Foghorn - Siren signalling the letter V. 60 seconds
Helipad - No
Open to the public - No
Inhabited - Yes

Cabo Villano

When it was built in 1896, Cabo Villano was the first electric lighthouse in Spain. The original generator no longer works, but carries a medal from the 1892 Paris Universal Exhibition. Cristina Fernández Pasantes, Antonio Alonso Ballester and Juan Dios Canosa are the keepers at this lighthouse, which is accessed by a covered passageway protecting them from the weather.

Cabo Finisterre

The ancients believed that the world ended beyond the Cabo Finisterre. The Death Coast started here and ran south, where the fog and sea mist could be impenetrable. Today, the north-south shipping routes pass by this large light, manned by Francisco Manuel Lijo Domínguez.

Region - Galicia
Position - 42°52'9"N - 9°16'3"W
Year of construction - 1853
Architect - Félix Uhagon
Height - 17 metres/56 feet
Height above sea level - 143 metres/469 feet
Visibility - 25 miles
Optics - Fresnel
Lights - 1 white flash. 5 seconds
Foghorn - 12 signals. 60 seconds
Helipad - No
Open to the public - No
Inhabited - Yes

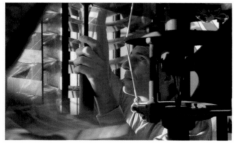

Region - Galicia
Position - 42°34'6"N - 9°05'4"W
Year of construction - 1854
Architect - Celedonio de Uribe
Height - 13 metres/43 feet
Height above sea level -
32 metres/105 feet

Visibility - 15 miles
Optics - Fresnel
Lights - 3 red flashes. 20 seconds
Foghorn - Siren signalling the letter O. 60 seconds
Helipad - No
Open to the public - No
Inhabited - Yes

Corrubedo

The Corrubedo lighthouse, where
the old meets the new...
The building, constructed in
1854, is covered with graffiti,
and the former keeper (now
retired) still comes to visit his
young successor, Juan Pablo
García Domínguez.

Isla de Sálvora

The west coast of Galicia is a labyrinth of rias (or inlets) dotted generously with reefs. Isla de Sálvora is a natural reserve, home to sea birds and wild horses.

Region - Galicia
Position - 42°27'9"N - 9°00'8"W
Year of construction - 1852
Engineer - Ramón Martínez Campos
Height - 16 metres/52 feet
Height above sea level - 40 metres/131 feet
Visibility - 21 miles
Optics - Fresnel
Lights - 4 white flashes (3 + 1). 20 seconds
Helipad - No
Open to the public - No
Inhabited - No

Region - Galicia
Position - 42°22'9"N - 8°56'2"W
Year of construction - 1865, 1926
Engineer - Rafael de la Cerda
Height - 12 metres/39 feet
Height above sea level - 127 metres/417 feet

Visibility - 25 miles
Optics - Fresnel
Lights - 4 white flashes. 24 seconds
Helipad - Yes
Open to the public - No
Inhabited - No

Isla Ons

Unlike Sálvora, Isla Ons
is lush and inhabited.
The lighthouse and its buildings
are remarkably elegant. Behind
them is the nautical labyrinth
formed by the Arosa ria, a true
inland sea. The light still runs
on oil.

Islas Cíes

Two islands form the Islas Cíes:
one is a popular place for Sunday
outings by the locals; the other
houses the lighthouse, which
signals the entrance to the great
Galician port. A steep, windy road
leads up to the lighthouse.

Region - Galicia
Position - 42°12'8"N - 8°54'9"W
Year of construction - 1853
Architect - Alejandro Olavarría
Height - 10 metres/33 feet
Height above sea level - 187 metres/614 feet
Visibility - 22 miles
Optics - Fresnel
Lights - 2 white flashes. 8 seconds
Helipad - No
Open to the public - No
Inhabited - No

Cabo Silleiro is the last Spanish lighthouse before Portugal. The keeper, Manuel Expósito Álvarez, loves sailing catamarans. He even constructed one at the tip of the deserted promontory (see page 162).

Cabo Silleiro

Region - Galicia
Position - 42°0' 6"N - 8°53'8"W
Year of construction - 1925
Engineer - Mauro Serret
Height - 30 metres/98 feet
Height above sea level - 85 metres/279 feet
Visibility - 24 miles
Optics - Fresnel
Lights - 3 white flashes (2+1). 15 seconds
Foghorn - Siren signalling the letter S. 30 seconds
Helipad - No
Open to the public - No
Inhabited - Yes

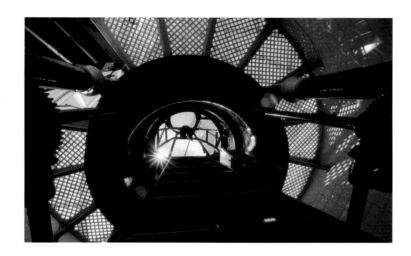

193

Cabo Higuer

Region - Basque country
Position - 43°23'6"N - 1°47'4"W
Year of construction - 1881
Architect - Lafarga
Height - 21 metres/69 feet
Height above sea level -
65 metres/213 feet

Visibility - 23 miles
Optics - Fresnel
Lights - 2 white flashes. 10 seconds
Helipad - No
Open to the public - No
Inhabited - Yes

Guetaria

Region - Basque country
Position - 43°18'6"N - 02°12'1"W
Year of construction - 1863
Architect - Manuel Estibaus
Height - 14 metres/46 feet
Height above sea level -
93 metres/305 feet

Visibility - 21 miles
Optics - Revolving light with reflectors
Lights - 4 white flashes. 15 seconds
Helipad - No
Open to the public - No
Inhabited - Yes

Eight different lighthouses, spread along the entire northern and western coast of Spain. There is one intruder among them: Cabo Lastres, the most recent, is the only one that does not have a traditional dome-shaped lantern.

Zumaya

Region - Basque country
Position - 43°18'1"N - 2°15'1"W
Year of construction - 1870
Architect - Inocencio de Elorza
Height - 10 metres/33 feet
Height above sea level -
41 metres/135 feet

Visibility - 12 miles
Optics - Fresnel
Lights - 4 occ. (1 and 3). 12 seconds
Helipad - No
Open to the public - No
Inhabited - Yes

Lequeitio

Region - Basque country
Position - 43°22'6"N - 2°30'6"W
Year of construction - 1862
Architect - Amado de Lazaro
Height - 13 metres/43 feet
Height above sea level -
46 metres/151 feet
Visibility - 17 miles

Optics - Fresnel
Lights - 4 white flashes (3 + 1).
20 seconds
Foghorn - Siren signalling the letter
L. 20 seconds
Helipad - No
Open to the public - No
Inhabited - No

Suances

Region - Cantabria
Position - 43°26'5"N - 4°02'6"W
Year of construction - 1863
Engineer - Romero
Height - 9 metres/30 feet
Height above sea level -
35 metres/115 feet

Visibility - 22 miles
Optics - Revolving light with reflectors
Lights - 3 white flashes (1+2).
24 seconds
Helipad - No
Open to the public - No
Inhabited - Yes

San Emeterio

Region - Asturias
Position - 43°24'0"N - 4°32'1"W
Year of construction - 1864
Engineer - Rafael de la Cerda
Height - 10 metres/33 feet
Height above sea level -
70 metres/230 feet

Visibility - 20 miles
Optics - Fresnel
Lights - White flash. 5 seconds
Helipad - No
Open to the public - No
Inhabited - Yes

Ribadesella

Region - Asturias
Position - 43°28'22"N - 5°4'59"W
Year of construction - 1861
Engineer - Francisco Pérez Muñoz
Height - 8 metres/26 feet
Height above sea level - 112 metres

Visibility - 21 miles
Optics - Fresnel
Lights - 3 white flashes. 12 seconds
Helipad - No
Open to the public - No
Inhabited - No

Lastres

Region - Asturias
Position - 43°32'1"N - 5°17'9"W
Year of construction - 1993
Height - 17.4 metres/57 feet
Height above sea level -
117.4 metres/385 feet
Date of automation - 1993

Visibility - 23 miles
Optics - Revolving light with reflectors
Lights - 0.30 seconds of light and
11.7 seconds of darkness. 12 seconds
Helipad - No
Open to the public - No
Inhabited - No

Candas

Region - Asturias
Position - 43°35'7"N - 5°47'7"W
Year of construction - 1917
Engineer - Jesús Goicoechea
Height - 12 metres/39 feet
Height above sea level -
40 metres/131 feet
Visibility - 13 miles

Optics - Fresnel
Lights - White, occulting
10 seconds (2+2+2+4 = 10)
Foghorn - Siren signalling the letter C.
43.5 seconds
Helipad - No
Open to the public - No
Inhabited - No

Avilés

Region - Asturias
Position - 43°35'44"N - 5°56'44"W
Year of construction - 1863
Height - 15 metres/49 feet
Height above sea level -
40 metres/131 feet
Visibility - 20 miles
Optics - Fresnel

Lights - White light surrounded by
red, 5-second occultations
Foghorn - Siren signalling the letter A.
30 seconds.
Helipad - No
Open to the public - No
Inhabited - Yes

Cudillero

Region - Asturias
Position - 43°34' 00"N - 6°2'15"W
Year of construction - 1858
Engineer - Javier Marquina
Height - 7.6 metres/25 feet
Height above sea level -
30.1 metres/99 feet
Visibility - 25 miles

Optics - Fresnel
Lights - 4 occultat
Foghorn - Siren si
D. 30 seconds
Helipad - No
Open to the public
Inhabited - No

Busto

Region - Asturias
Position - 43°34'49"N - 6°28'11"W
Year of construction - 1858
Engineer - Javier Marquina
Height - 10 metres/33 feet
Height above sea level -
73 metres/240 feet

Visibility - 21 mile
Optics - Fresnel
Lights - 4 flashes.
Helipad - No
Open to the public
Inhabited - Yes

Tapia de Casariego

Region - Asturias
Position - 43°34'27"N - 6°56'47"W
Year of construction - 1859, 1962
Engineer - Javier Marquina
Height - 8 metres/26 feet
Height above sea level -
24 metres/79 feet

Visibility - 25 mile
Optics - Fresnel
Lights - 3 white f
Helipad - No
Open to the public
Inhabited - No

San Ciprián

Region - Galicia
Position - 43°42'1"N - 7°26'1"W
Year of construction - 1864, 1983
Height - 14 metres/46 feet
Height above sea level -
41 metres/135 feet

Visibility - 15 mile
Optics - Fresnel
Lights - 4 white f
Helipad - No
Open to the public
Inhabited - Yes

Roncadoira

Region - Galicia
Position - 43°44'1"N - 7°31'5"W
Year of construction - 1986
Height - 14 metres/46 feet
Height above sea level -
94 metres/308 feet

Visibility - 21 mile
Lights - 1 white fl
Helipad - No
Open to the public
Inhabited - No

Isla Coelleira

Region - Galicia
Position - 43°45'5"N - 7°37'8"W
Year of construction - 1864
Engineer - Marcelo Sánchez Novellán
Height - 7 metres/23 feet
Height above sea level -
89 metres/292 feet

Visibility - 8 miles
Optics - Fresnel
Lights - 4 white f
Helipad - No
Open to the public
Inhabited - No

Candelaria

Region - Galicia
Position - 43°42'7"N - 8°02'8"W
Year of construction - 1954
Height - 9 metres/30 feet
Height above sea level -
89 metres/292 feet
Visibility - 21 miles

Optics - Revolving light with reflectors
Lights - 4 white flashes (3 + 1).
24 seconds
Helipad - No
Open to the public - No
Inhabited - Yes

Frouseira

Region - Galicia
Position - 43°37'1"N - 8°11'3"W
Height - 30 metres/98 feet
Height above sea level -
75 metres/246 feet
Visibility - 20 miles

Optics - Fresnel
Lights - 5 white flashes. 20 seconds
Helipad - No
Open to the public - No
Inhabited - No

Prior

Region - Galicia
Position - 43°34'1"N - 8°18'9"W
Year of construction - 1916
Engineer - Salvador López Miño
Height - 7 metres/23 feet
Height above sea level -
107 metres/351 feet
Visibility - 22 miles

Optics - Fresnel
Lights - 3 white flashes (2 and 1).
15 seconds
Foghorn - Siren signalling the letter P.
25 seconds
Helipad - No
Open to the public - No
Inhabited - No

Prioriño

Region - Galicia
Position - 43°27'6"N - 8°20'3"W
Year of construction - 1854
Height - 5 metres/16 feet
Height above sea level -
36 metres/118 feet

Visibility - 23 miles
Optics - Fresnel
Lights - 1 white flash. 5 seconds
Helipad - No
Open to the public - No
Inhabited - Yes

Touriñán

Region - Galicia
Position - 43°03'2"N - 9°17'9"W
Year of construction - 1898, 1981
Height - 11 metres/36 feet
Height above sea level -
65 metres/213 feet
Visibility - 23 miles

Optics - Fresnel
Lights - 3 white flashes (2 + 1).
15 seconds
Helipad - No
Open to the public - No
Inhabited - No

Punta Insúa

Region - Galicia
Position - 42°46'3"N - 9°07'6"W
Year of construction - 1921
Architect - Salvador López Miño
Height - 14 metres/46 feet
Height above sea level -
27 metres/88 feet
Visibility - 15 miles white,
14 miles red

Optics - Fresnel
Lights - 3 occultations (1+2).
20 seconds
Helipad - No
Open to the public - No
Inhabited - No

The Iberian Lighthouses

Portugal and Andalusia, our Journey's End

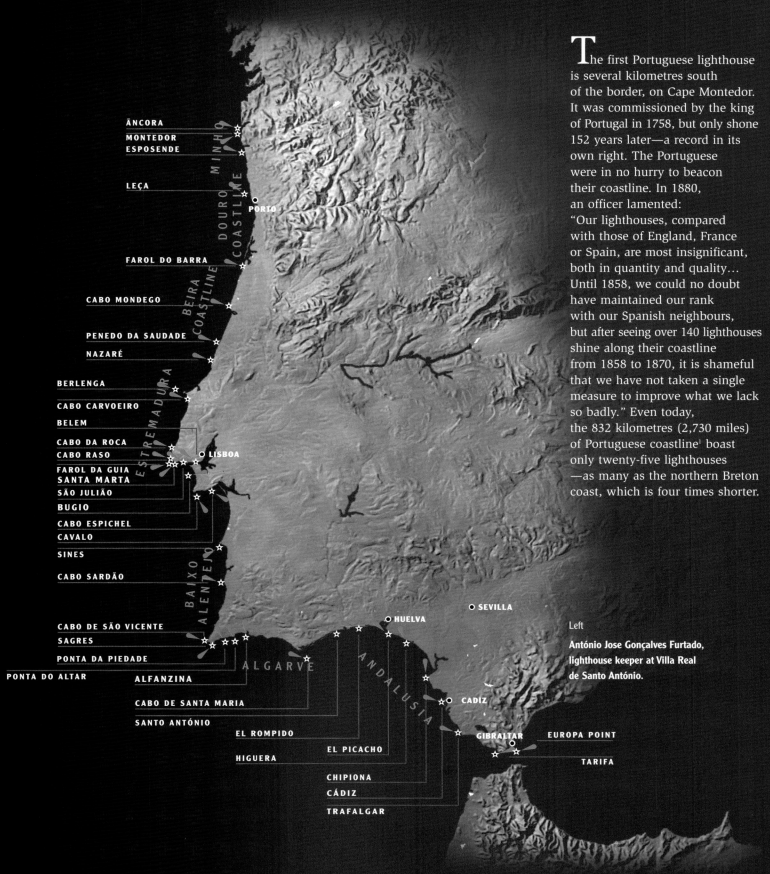

ÂNCORA
MONTEDOR
ESPOSENDE

LEÇA
PORTO

FAROL DO BARRA

CABO MONDEGO

PENEDO DA SAUDADE
NAZARÉ

BERLENGA
CABO CARVOEIRO
BELEM
CABO DA ROCA
CABO RASO
FAROL DA GUIA
SANTA MARTA
SÃO JULIÃO
BUGIO
CABO ESPICHEL
CAVALO

SINES

CABO SARDÃO

CABO DE SÃO VICENTE
SAGRES
PONTA DA PIEDADE
PONTA DO ALTAR
ALFANZINA

CABO DE SANTA MARIA
SANTO ANTÓNIO
EL ROMPIDO
HIGUERA
EL PICACHO
CHIPIONA
CÁDIZ
TRAFALGAR

LISBOA

MINHO COASTLINE
DOURO COASTLINE
BEIRA COASTLINE
ESTREMADURA
BAIXO ALENTEJO
ALGARVE
ANDALUSIA

SEVILLA
HUELVA
CADIZ
GIBRALTAR
EUROPA POINT
TARIFA

The first Portuguese lighthouse
is several kilometres south
of the border, on Cape Montedor.
It was commissioned by the king
of Portugal in 1758, but only shone
152 years later—a record in its
own right. The Portuguese
were in no hurry to beacon
their coastline. In 1880,
an officer lamented:
"Our lighthouses, compared
with those of England, France
or Spain, are most insignificant,
both in quantity and quality…
Until 1858, we could no doubt
have maintained our rank
with our Spanish neighbours,
but after seeing over 140 lighthouses
shine along their coastline
from 1858 to 1870, it is shameful
that we have not taken a single
measure to improve what we lack
so badly." Even today,
the 832 kilometres (2,730 miles)
of Portuguese coastline[1] boast
only twenty-five lighthouses
—as many as the northern Breton
coast, which is four times shorter.

Left

**António Jose Gonçalves Furtado,
lighthouse keeper at Villa Real
de Santo António.**

Ancient Lusitania had a complex maritime history. Its origins were Phoenician, and there are still large, sharp-angled "Phoenician-style" fishing boats with no central keel, the bottom of which is held together with strong cross boards that strengthen the hull. These are the ancestors of the dory (which the Americans claim as their own invention). The Phoenicians evangelised Ireland, but their adventurous streak abated under Moorish domination (711-1249), although it did not protect them from Viking incursions. The latter left their mark, as can be seen by traditional boats in the north of Portugal, directly inspired by the Viking longships. Later, Portugal became a great maritime power, with conquests as far as Macao to the east and America to the west. Unfortunately, the country was annexed by Spain from 1580 to 1640, and spent years fighting this larger neighbour. Several centuries later, Napoleon invaded (1807-1811). This political turbulence was hardly propitious to maritime expansion. This explains, at least in part, why the age of the lighthouse began without the Portuguese, whose main concern was to prevent, rather than facilitate, access to their coasts.

Cádiz

Bugio, at the mouth of the Tage, served the same purpose as Cordouan on the Gironde—except that there was no fire in the wooden fort (built c. 1570). A stone structure replaced the wooden one, but it became a lighthouse only in 1775, 150 years after its construction. Yet Bugio deserves a place of honour in lighthouse history, because it was without doubt the very first example of reef architecture. To construct this circular fort, some 25 metres (82 feet) in diameter, on a reef

Trafalgar

which was submerged at high tide, the stones had to be embedded into each other with metal inserts and tar. The fact that it took fifty-six years gives some indication of the difficulty of this Herculean task. It was started in 1590 by the Spanish engineer Leonardo Turriano and finished in 1646 by his son João. This would have made them the first dynasty of lighthouse builders (well before the Stevensons of Scotland, the Halpins of Ireland or the Douglasses of England) had their masterpiece originally been something other than a fort.

Other fortresses also added lighthouses somewhat after the fact. These included the fort of Cabo Raso, facing Bugio; and a little farther, the fortress of São Julião; then Esposende and Âncora, not far from the northern border; and Cavalo to the south. The artificial island of Bugio, however, is the only major landmark in the history of lighthouses: it can be ranked among the three greatest, along with Cordouan and Eddystone.

The lighthouse of São Vicente, inaugurated in 1515, the year of the battle of Marignan, is located at the southwestern tip of Portugal. This structure marks a turning point in more ways than one: the coastline to the north is rocky for hundreds of kilometres, but here it becomes an interlacing network of beaches and lagoons. To follow the coastline, you have to head east, which leads towards Spain.

The Atlantic Rim can be compared to a gigantic tree: Scotland, Ireland and England are the leaves; France is the branches (of which the main one is Cordouan); and Spain and Portugal form a smooth trunk with no knots or bumps, with the exception of two exceptional lighthouses, the Torre de Hércules and the fort of Bugio. Rounding São Vicente, we finally reach the roots.

In the days before aviation, the entire coast was in the hands of those who controlled the area around São Vicente. This was not only a place of strategic importance for traffic between the Mediterranean and the north of Europe. At a time when it was difficult to steer the great sailing ships to windward—which was the case until the advent of steamships—ships had to sail down the Portuguese coast to reach the trade winds, before launching out towards the Americas. They all, therefore, passed by São Vicente.

In 1492, for example, Christopher Columbus set sail with three caravels from Huelva, at the far end of this bay, in search of a passage to India, only to discover America instead.

When navigation was regulated by the winds, hardly any site was more strategic than this huge bay between the tips of Portugal and Africa. Known as Trafalgar, it would be the site of one of the greatest sea battles ever.

Chipiona

In 1805, Horatio Nelson lost his life winning the decisive naval battle of Trafalgar—but the bay in fact belongs to the mountains of central Spain, of Toledo and Ronda, and the rivers that flow down them: the Guadiana, the Odiel, the Rio Tinto, the Guadalquivir and the Guadalete. In a few thousand years, these rivers will fill Trafalgar with their alluvium. The noble city of Seville, a sea port in Moorish times, is already landlocked some 70 kilometres (230 miles) inland. There are no reefs and no rock lighthouses. The existing lights signal the estuaries of the Guadiana, which separates Spain and Portugal; of the great delta formed by the Odiel and the Tinto, site of the port of Huelva (where Columbus set sail); and of the Guadalete. The estuary of the latter is not silted up like that of the Guadalquivir, and is home to Cádiz, the port of Jeréz de la Frontera, birthplace of sherry.

Here stood an 89-metre (292-foot) tower where fires were lit to guide sailors, under a huge colonnade supporting a statue of Hercules. This second "Tower of Hercules", built by the Romans, was destroyed by the Arabs in 1146. In about 1400, it was replaced by a fort with walls nearly 6 metres (20 feet) thick. The fort had so many elements added to it over the

The coast rises up into what looks like an enormous stump growing out of the earth. This is "the mountain of Tariq", "Gibel Tariq".

years that by the mid-eighteenth century it had reached a height of nearly 50 metres (164 feet). Yet one hundred years later, it was gone, a victim of the Spanish-American war of 1898. The imposing building stuck out like a sore thumb on this flat, sandy coastline, announcing the presence of Cádiz to all and sundry. In case the lighthouse helped the enemy find the town, this historic building was demolished—in vain, as the Americans never attacked Cádiz. When peace returned, a metal lighthouse was constructed, but it was designed to be dismantled, just in case. But it still stands.

From this point, the coast rises up into what looks like an enormous stump growing out of the earth. This is "the mountain of Tariq", "Gibel Tariq": Gibraltar, the rock at the base of the Atlantic Rim. But the roots of Lighthouse Country spread farther east, as far as the island of Pharos where Sostratus of Cnidos built the biggest lighthouse of all time. The lights of Tangiers are visible opposite Gibraltar. To the east are ancient lands, while the west, south and north were the directions taken by explorers of the past, Greek merchants, Phoenicians and Romans. Modern maritime history begins here. And here, at the Pillars of Hercules, our journey ends.

1 Not including the Azores, Madeira and Macao, of course.

Europa Point

The light colored stones cliffs of Cabo Espichel, south of Lisbon.

Leça

When the Leça lighthouse was constructed in 1926 at the mouth of the Douro River, the refinery did not yet exist. Until 1961, Portuguese lighthouse keepers were trained here.

Region - Douro littoral
Position - 41°12'58"N - 8°42'48"W
Year of construction - 1926
Height - 40 metres/131 feet
Height above sea level - 116 metres/380 feet
Date of automation - 1964

Visibility - 43 miles
Optics - Fresnel
Lights - 3 flashes. 14 seconds
Helipad - No
Open to the public - No
Inhabited - Yes

Region - Beira littoral
Position - 40°38'47"N - 8°44'80"W
Year of construction - 1885
Height - 49 metres/160 feet
Height above sea level - 66 metres/216 feet
Date of automation - 1950
Visibility - 28 miles
Optics - Fresnel
Lights - 4 flashes. 13 seconds
Foghorn - compressed air
Helipad - No
Open to the public - Yes (around the lighthouse)
Inhabited - Yes

Farol do Barra

This lighthouse signals the entrance to the huge Aveiro ria. Like Leça, it was fitted with an elevator in the 1950s. Farol do Barra was the first Portuguese lighthouse to be illustrated on a stamp.

Cabo Mondego

When this lighthouse was built in 1857, it used 1,307,000 litres of olive oil per year! It was torn down so that the quarries (in the background) could be extended, reconstructed in 1917, and almost burnt down during the 1993 forest fires.

Region - Beira littoral
Position - 40°11'36"N - 8°54'24"W
Year of construction - 1857, 1917
Ingénieur - Guadencio Fontana
Height - 10 metres
Height above sea level - 102 metres
Date of automation - 1988
Visibility - 29 miles
Optics - Fresnel
Lights - 1 flash. 5 seconds
Helipad - No
Open to the public - No
Inhabited - Yes

FAROL
DO
CABO MONDEGO

206

Nazaré

Nazaré point was defended by a small fort: a light was installed in 1903 to signal the entrance to this port where lamparo has been fished for three centuries. At night, the swinging lamps on the boats echo the light from the lantern's lighthouse.

Region - Estremadura
Position - 39°36'34"N - 9°05'03"W
Year of construction - 1903
Height - 785 metres/26 feet
Height above sea level - 50 metres/164 feet
Date of automation - 1986
Visibility - 15 miles
Optics - Fresnel
Lights - Fixed red light
Helipad - No
Open to the public - Yes
Inhabited - No

Berlenga

By the end of spring, the vegetation on the Berlenga islands has been replaced by the fine down of birds; you'd almost think it had snowed. A natural phosphorescent tunnel crosses through the main island. The small fort, which is no longer used, once defended the port of Peniche.

Region - Estremadura
Position - 39°24'99''N - 9°30'47''W
Year of construction - 1836
Ingénieur - Guadencio Fontana & André Proença Vieira
Height - 22 metres/72 feet
Height above sea level - 121 metres/ 396 feet
Date of automation - 1985
Visibility - 27 miles
Optics - Fresnel
Lights - 3 flashes. 20 seconds
Helipad - No
Open to the public - No
Inhabited - Yes

Region - Estremadura
Position - 39°21'54"N - 9°22'45"W
Year of construction - 1758
Engineer - Castenheira das Neves
Height - 23.70 metres/78 feet
Height above sea level - 55.52 metres/
180 feet

Date of automation - 1988
Visibility - 15 miles
Optics - Fresnel
Lights - 3 red flashes. 15 seconds
Helipad - No
Open to the public - No
Inhabited - Yes

Cabo Carvoeiro

Carvoeiro is situated opposite Berlenga, and the two lighthouses are aligned to facilitate the entrance into Peniche. When the olive-oil system of lighting was abandoned in 1923 in favour of petroleum, consumption dropped by 45 percent.

Cabo da Roca

Cabo da Roca is the westernmost point of the European continent. A lighthouse was first constructed here in 1772; the current lighthouse dates from 1846. The keeper, Edgar Bentes, climbs this small staircase (below left) to reach the lantern.

Region - Estremadura
Position - 38°46'99''N - 9°29'75''W
Year of construction - 1772
Ingénieur - D. J. Mendoza e Rios
Height - 23.50 metres/75 feet
Height above sea level - 165 metres/541 feet
Date of automation - 1980
Visibility - 26 miles
Optics - Fresnel
Lights - 2 white flashes. 3 seconds
Foghorn - Yes
Helipad - No
Open to the public - No
Inhabited - Yes

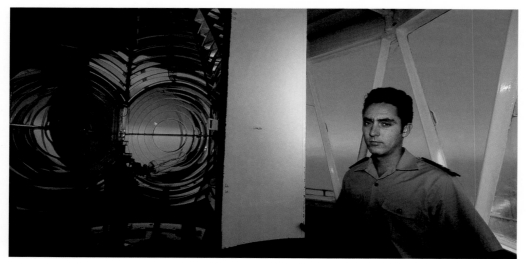

Region - Estremadura
Position - 38°42'06"N - 9°25'17"W
Year of construction - 1868
Height - 12 metres/40 feet
Height above sea level - 25 metres/82 feet
Date of automation - 1980
Visibility - 15 miles
Optics - Fresnel
Lights - Red, 1 flash. 6 seconds
Helipad - No
Open to the public - No
Inhabited - Yes

Santa Marta

The Santa Marta lighthouse marks the entrance to the Tagus River. It existed before the nearby hotel was constructed, but it had to be raised in 1936 so that it would stand out from nearby structures.

Region - Estremadura
Position - 38°39'70''N - 9°17'85''W
Year of construction - 1775
Ingénieur - Gaudencio Fontana
Height - 26.13 metres/85 feet
Height above sea level - 28 metres/
91 feet
Date of automation - 1981
Visibility - 21 miles
Optics - Fresnel
Lights - 5 flashes. 5 seconds
Foghorn - Yes
Helipad - No
Open to the public - No
Inhabited - No

Bugio

The small fort of Bugio was the first building constructed on a reef that is submerged at high tide. It took 56 years to build and had to be reinforced eight times—most recently in June of 1998. There is also a lighthouse in Lisbon proper (right), but it is a fake!

Region - Alentejo
Position - 38°24'84''N - 9°12'90''W
Year of construction - 1790
Height - 30.70 metres/98 feet
Height above sea level - 168 metres/551 feet
Date of automation - 1980
Visibility - 26 miles
Optics - Fresnel
Lights - 1 flash. 4 seconds
Helipad - No
Open to the public - No
Inhabited - Yes

Cabo Espichel

In the fifteenth century, on the site of the current lighthouse (constructed in 1790), stood a tower that was illuminated by torches and maintained by monks from a nearby abbey (see also pages 202-203).

Region - Baixo Alentejo
Position - 37°35'82'' N - 8°48' 89''W
Year of construction - 1915
Engineer - Perreira Da Silva
Height - 14 metres/46 feet
Height above sea level - 68 metres/ 223 feet
Date of automation - 1984
Visibility - 23 miles
Optics - Fresnel
Lights - 3 flashes. 15 seconds
Helipad - No
Open to the public - No
Inhabited - Yes

Cabo Sardão

From the sea, the access to Cabo Sardão is forbidding; it is no less difficult by land, and the Portuguese Lighthouse and Beacon administration hired a messenger to hand-deliver mail and messages.

Cabo de São Vicente

Cabo de São Vicente is the oldest lighthouse in Portugal. Monks lit a fire for the first time here in 1515. The monastery grew, and a new tower was built in 1846, which was equipped with an enormous lens, 4 metres (13 feet) high and 1.33 metres (4 feet) in diameter.

Region - Algarve
Position - 37°01'28"N - 8°59'72"W
Year of construction - 1846
Engineer - Perreira da Silva
Height - 25.70 metres/88 feet
Height above sea level - 86 metres/ 282 feet
Date of automation - 1982
Visibility - 32 miles
Optics - Fresnel
Lights - 1 flash. 5 seconds
Foghorn - Yes
Helipad - No
Open to the public - Yes (around the lighthouse)
Inhabited - Yes

Sagres

The Sagres peninsula could not be taken from the sea, and a small fort was constructed to defend this deserted rock from an enemy arriving from the mainland—but one wonders why? The lighthouse was added in 1894, and is now monitored by São Vicente.

Region - Algarve	Visibility - 11 miles
Position - 36°59'5"N - 8°56'88"W	Optics - Fresnel
Year of construction - 1894	Lights - Fixed red light
Height - 13 metres/42 feet	Helipad - No
Height above sea level - 53 metres/173 feet	Open to the public - No
Date of automation - 1982	Inhabited - No

Ponta da Piedade

Region - Algarve
Position - 37°04'74''N - 8°40'09''W
Year of construction - 1913
Height - 8 metres/26 feet
Height above sea level - 51 metres/167 feet
Date of automation - 1998

Visibility - 20 miles
Optics - Fresnel
Lights - 1 flash. 7 seconds
Helipad - No
Open to the public - No
Inhabited - Yes

An old chapel once stood at Ponta da Piedade, occupying what little land is available. The highest religious authorities in Portugal had to intervene before a lighthouse could be constructed here.

Alfanzina

This lighthouse, similar in design to that of Carvoeiro, stands high atop the cliffs of the Algarve. It is part of a series of five lighthouses on the southwest tip of Portugal, but it is not, as opposed to the two preceding lighthouses, monitored from São Vicente.

Region - Algarve
Position - 37°05'11"N - 8°26'48"W
Year of construction - 1920
Height - 16 metres/52 feet
Height above sea level - 63 metres/
206 feet
Date of automation - 1984
Visibility - 29 miles
Optics - Fresnel
Lights - 2 flashes. 11 seconds
Helipad - No
Open to the public - No
Inhabited - Yes

Cabo de Santa Maria

After miles of cliffs, the coastline opens up to form the Faro lagoon. The entrance is marked by the Santa Maria lighthouse. In 1996, the lantern had to be completely restored.

Region - Algarve
Position - 36°58'38"N - 7°51'81"W
Year of construction - 1851
Engineer - Guadencio Fontana
Height - 35.55 metres/114 feet
Height above sea level - 50 metres/ 164 feet
Date of automation - 1996
Visibility - 25 miles
Optics - Fresnel
Lights - 4 flashes. 17 seconds
Foghorn - Yes
Helipad - No
Open to the public - No
Inhabited - Yes

Santo António

This is the last Portuguese lighthouse before the Spanish border. António José Gonçalves Furtado holds an old lamp (bottom left) and poses with his colleague Joaquim José Pentrado (left).

Region - Algarve
Position - 37°11'12"N - 7°24'91"W
Year of construction - 1923
Engineer - Ricardo Peyroteu & Domingos Tasso de Figueiredo
Height - 40 metres/131 feet
Height above sea level - 52 metres/ 170 feet
Date of automation - 1986
Visibility - 26 miles
Optics - Fresnel
Lights - 1 flash. 6 seconds
Foghorn - Yes
Helipad - No
Open to the public - No
Inhabited - Yes

El Rompido

With El Rompido we are back in Spain, as evidenced by the dome-shaped lantern. The new lighthouse was constructed in 1975 behind the older one, which was too low and not powerful enough.

Region - Andalusia
Position - 37°13'2"N - 7°07'5"W
Year of construction - 1861, 1975
Engineer - Angel Mayo
Height - 29 metres/95 feet
Height above sea level - 43 metres/141 feet
Visibility - 24 miles
Optics - Revolving reflectors
Lights - 2 white flashes. 10 seconds
Helipad - No
Open to the public - No
Inhabited - No

El Picacho

This photograph is a dream come true: Francisco Cano Garracho had always lived at the lighthouse, but had never successfully passed the administrative examination to become a keeper. As the official lighthouse keeper had just died, Garracho was our guide, and became lighthouse keeper for a day.

Region - Andalusia
Position - 37°08'2"N - 6°49'5"W
Year of construction - 1901
Height - 25 metres/82 feet
Height above sea level - 52 metres/170 feet
Visibility - 25 miles
Optics - Fresnel
Lights - 6 white flashes (2+4). 30 seconds
Helipad - No
Open to the public - No
Inhabited - Yes

Chipiona

FARO DE CHIPIONA

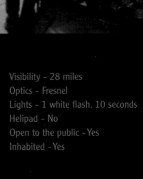

The Chipiona lighthouse, built in 1867, is one of the most beautiful in Spain, with a patio protected by a glass pyramid. Pedro Ernesto climbs this splendid staircase to attend to the lantern's maintenance.

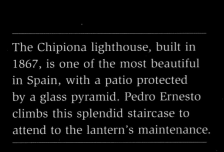

Region - Andalusia
Position - 36°44'3"N - 6°26'4"W
Year of construction - 1867
Architect - Eduardo Saavedra
Height - 63 metres/206 feet
Height above sea level - 69 metres/226 feet

Visibility - 28 miles
Optics - Fresnel
Lights - 1 white flash. 10 seconds
Helipad - No
Open to the public - Yes
Inhabited - Yes

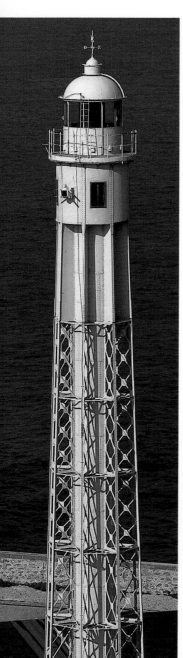

This metal lighthouse, built in 1913, signals the entrance to Cádiz— but a tower (demolished in the 19th century) had existed since ancient times.

Francisco Javier Cercas De Castro lives a fairly isolated life with his family in the middle of this fort, which is used as an artillery school by the Spanish navy.

Cádiz

Region - Andalusia
Position - 36°31'8"N - 6°18'9"W
Year of construction - 1913
Architect - Rafael de la Cerda
Height - 35 meters/115 feet
Height above sea level - 39 m. / 127 f.
Visibility - 25 miles
Optics - Fresnel

Lights - 2 white flashes. 10 seconds
Foghorn - Siren signalling the letter N.
20 seconds
Helipad - No
Open to the public - No
Inhabited - Yes

Trafalgar

Region - Andalusia
Position - 36°11'0"N - 6°02'0"W
Year of construction - 1862
Architect - Eduardo Saavedra
Height - 34 metres/111 feet
Height above sea level - 51 metres/167 feet

Visibility - 29 miles
Optics - Fresnel
Lights - 3 white flashes (1+2). 15 seconds
Helipad - No
Open to the public - No
Inhabited - Yes

The Trafalgar lighthouse was built in two different periods. The central shaft and the lantern date from 1862, but the tower reinforcements were added in the 1930s.

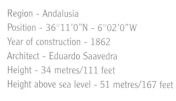

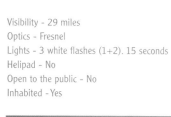

Region - Andalusia (Gibraltar)
Position - 36°06'67''N - 05°20'62''W
Year of construction - 1841
Height - 19 metres/62 feet
Height above sea level - 49 metres/160 feet
Date of automation - 1994
Visibility - 21 miles white, 17 miles red
Optics - Fresnel
Lights - White and red
Foghorn - 1 sound. 20 seconds
Helipad - No
Open to the public - No
Inhabited - Yes

The Europa Point lighthouse
is on Gibraltar, a British colony,
but the nearby mosque reminds
us that Europe ends here, as does
our trip. On the other side of the
Strait lies Africa.

Europa Point

231

Montedor

Region - Minho
Position - 41°44'97"N - 8°52'33"W
Year of construction - 1908
Engineer - Schulzt Xavier
Height - 22.39 metres/72 feet
Height above sea level - 103 metres/
337 feet

Date of automation - 1987
Visibility - 22 to 26 miles
Optics - Fresnel
Lights - 2 flashes. 9.5 seconds
Helipad - No
Open to the public - No
Inhabited - Yes

These lighthouses are Portuguese, except the last one (which is Spanish). A coast without lighthouses is as hard to imagine as a village without a church tower.

Esposende

Region - Minho
Position - 41°37'41"N - 8°47'36"W
Year of construction - 1922
Height - 7 metres/23 feet
Height above sea level - 21 metres/
69 feet
Date of automation - 1938

Visibility - 21 miles
Optics - Fresnel
Lights - Single flash. 5 seconds
Foghorn - Yes
Helipad - No
Open to the public - No
Inhabited - Yes

Penedo da Saudade

Region - Beira litoral
Position - 39°45'75"N - 8°54'24"W
Year of construction - 1912
Engineer - Perreira Da Silva
Height - 26.40 metres/85 feet
Height above sea level - 55 metres/
180 feet

Date of automation - 1980
Visibility - 30 miles
Optics - Fresnel
Lights - 2 flashes. 15 seconds
Helipad - No
Open to the public - No
Inhabited - Yes

Cabo Raso

Region - Estramadura
Position - 38°42'64"N - 9°29'06"W
Year of construction - 1894
Ingénieur - M. Castanheira das Neves
Height - 16 metres
Height above sea level - 23 metres
Date of automation - 1984

Visibility - 20 miles
Optics - Fresnel
Lights - Fixed red
Foghorn - Yes
Helipad - No
Open to the public - No
Inhabited - No

Farol da Guia

Region - Estremadura
Position - 38°41'81"N - 9°26'70"W
Year of construction - 1758
Height - 26.40 metres/85 feet
Height above sea level - 58 metres/
190 feet
Date of automation - 1982

Visibility - 21 miles
Optics - Fresnel
Lights - Fixed red
Helipad - No
Open to the public - No
Inhabited - Yes

São Julião

Region - Estremadura
Position - 38°40'54"N - 9°19'43"W
Year of construction - 1775, 1848
Height - 36.50 metres/118 feet
Height above sea level - 42 metres/
137 feet
Date of automation - 1980

Visibility - 14 miles
Optics - Fresnel
Lights - 1 white flash. 5 seconds
Helipad - No
Open to the public - No
Inhabited - No

Sines

Region - Baixo Alentejo
Position - 37°58'88"N - 8°52'75"W
Year of construction - 1880
Height - 22 metres/72 feet
Height above sea level - 50 metres/
164 feet
Date of automation - 1919

Visibility - 15 miles
Optics - Fresnel
Lights - 1 occultation. 5 seconds
Helipad - No
Open to the public - No
Inhabited - Yes

Ponta do Altar

Region - Algarve
Position - 37°06'25"N - 8°31'10"W
Year of construction - 1893
Height - 8.10 metres/26 feet
Height above sea level - 32 metres/
104 feet
Date of automation - 1983

Visibility - 14 miles
Optics - Fresnel
Lights - 1 red flash. 5 seconds
Helipad - No
Open to the public - No
Inhabited - No

Higuera

Region - Andalusia
Position - 37°00'6"N - 6°34'1"W
Year of construction - 1985-1989
Architect - Rafael Giménez Roig
Height - 24 metres/78 feet
Height above sea level - 47 metres/
154 feet

Visibility - 20 miles
Optics - Revolving reflective lights
Lights - 3 white flashes. 20 seconds
Helipad - No
Open to the public - No
Inhabited - No

Gale warning at La Jument, which signals the Fromveur passage.

There was nothing about the area in which I grew up that could predispose me to take an interest in the sea, but we spent family holidays in La Trinité-sur-Mer starting in 1951. From the channel, we could see the distant beam of Goulphar sweeping the horizon, although Belle-Île was 25 [nautical] miles away. It was the first lighthouse I ever visited, and the first time I ever saw a Fresnel lens. I was nine or ten at the time.

The first lighthouse I encountered when sailing was Teignouse in Quiberon Bay, and at that time it was inhabited. We often sailed past it, and I remember the keepers waving to us. Sometimes they were maintaining the light, and at other times we saw them fishing for bass. I found their lifestyle most appealing.

But the real shock, the time when my childhood dream turned into adult fascination, was when I first sailed round the French coast, in 1983. This coast-hugging voyage, from Dunkerque to Menton, was my first real opportunity to get a measure of French light-houses. Since then, I have photographed every single lighthouse I've seen! I have photographed them on every continent, and even as far as the southernmost tip of Tasmania, on the islet of Maatsuyker, which is four hours by helicopter from Hobart—and home to the last light-house keeper of the southern hemisphere.

But French lighthouses were still my reference, and I only began to revise my opinion when I started my work on the maritime heritage of Celtic countries in 1995. In Scotland and Ireland, I discovered lighthouses that were not monuments, like the French ones, but functional tools. I also encountered organisations and people with different approaches, who encouraged me to compile this inventory of the lighthouses along the west coast of our old continent, an area we now call the Atlantic Rim.

My aim was to compile a record, with no pretensions or artistic concessions; an end-of-century inventory, such as Richelieu commissioned from the Guild of Naval Painters, a body he established to create a visual record of our maritime history.

In terms of cost and time, it was an unreasonable undertaking. A partner had to be found, and fortunately, the Crédit Maritime was quick to appreciate the scope of the operation and to fund it accordingly. Our company, Pêcheur d'images, also invested in

My aim was to compile a record, with no pretensions or artistic concessions; an end-of-century inventory, such as Richelieu commissioned from the Guild of Naval Painters, a body he established to create a visual record of our maritime history.

the project for three years, to cover the 10,000 kilometres (6,200 miles) of coastline viewed from land, sea and helicopter. Today, I regret that I did not start this project earlier; our photos would have borne better witness to the keepers' daily occupations. We had the privilege, however, of being present during the final moments of the last keeper's presence on the last inhabited lighthouses in Scotland.

Guillaume and I worked with the kind of complicity and partnership one would expect from a father and son. We shared the work between us geographically: I visited all the lighthouses from the Shetlands to Cordouan, and Guillaume visited those from the Gironde to Gibraltar. But the most unforgettable aspect of the whole adventure was looking down at the lights from a helicopter, all the way from Muckle Flugga to Gibraltar: 120 hours in every type of weather conditions and in all seasons, even when we were stranded for five days in Galway, unable to take off due to fog.

Our most treasured memory was the ten days spent aboard the *Pharos*, the Northern Lights' boat, in the middle of winter. We ran into the legendary Highland storms, which was surely the best way of getting to know the world of Scottish light-houses. Our quarters were the Commissioners' cabins and private lounges. One day, we asked our chief steward to invite the captain and first officer to dine at our table. The chef suggested menus and let us choose the wine. Our hosts arrived in uniform, bearing gifts for us—as guests aboard their own ship.

After this wonderful voyage of discovery—of other people, other places, other maritime cultures—there is one question I ask myself: if, as Daniel Charles says, "lighthouses were born in the age of steam (...) their usefulness expired with the advent of satellites and computers", and if the Ministry of Transport has other priorities than the preservation of this patrimony, shouldn't the Ministry of Culture be made responsible for our lighthouses (like Cordouan), so that this heritage will not be lost at sea? As Tabarly put it so well: "The French are landsmen, but they do have coasts."

He might have added, "and lighthouses". But when you see the damaged roof of the Triagoz lighthouse, you can't help wondering: "For how much longer?"

Email: philip@plisson.com
Site: www.plisson.com

La Teignouse in Quiberon Bay.

Acknowledgments

If you liked this work, we would like you to know that we are indebted to the many men and women who worked alongside us in pursuit of this adventure:

The man of all trades, who was always ready for anything: our assistant Christophe Le Potier, who was responsible for the production of these images and was able to create a close relationship with the people who run the lighthouses and beacons in the countries we visited. He also kept track of all the technical information in this book, in conjunction with Anne Provost of the foreign rights department of Pêcheur d'images.

The walking encyclopedia for our maritime information: Daniel Charles, who agreed to show us the history of pharology, a fast-changing field today.

Our second eye, Daniel Manoury, who has worked with us for ten years. With his helicopter and his talent, he took us to the heart of our subject, day and night, in calm weather and in storms. We owe him for the most spectacular images we were able to capture.

Our gentleman pilot, Eric Oger, accompanied us during our aerial work in Scotland, Ireland and on the Iberian coast. Austere and discreet, he could have come from an elite corps assigned to ensure our safety.

Our financial partner, Crédit Maritime, which provided the funds to match our ambitions, and Elf Aquitaine, which accompanied us in our Celtic adventure.

Our friend from Ouessant, Jean-Michel Malgorn, son and grandson of lighthouse keepers, who provided two of the images in this book, on pages 120 and 128.

Our field assistants, Antonia Small for Scotland, Miguel Rosado-Boulet for Galicia, Bertrand Martins for Portugal, Olivier Chamaillard, one of Guillaume's friends, and our Scottish friend, Neil Corbasson.

For weather forecasts, Météo France and its marine forecasting service in Toulouse, which provided us with precise information throughout all our travels.

The best of the best, Fuji Film France, for the panoramic images, and our friends at Canon, who have supported our work for more than fifteen years.

Our publisher, Éditions du Chêne, directed by Isabelle Jendron, a Brittany sailor with whom we share the same language and the same emotions.

Expertise from Nantes, by the design agency Vu Par…, particularly Goretti, who designed the layout of this book. Master printers Jean-Paul and Pierre Le Govic, who were responsible for the color reproduction and printing of this adventure, as for our five earlier books.

SCOTLAND

With special thanks to Her Royal Highness, Princess Anne, patron of the Northern Lighthouse Board. During a royal visit to Fair Isle to celebrate the automation of the last inhabited lighthouse in Scotland, the princess requested that I be the only representative of the media to record the events of this day. A very great thanks to Lorna Grieve, NLB Information officer, our intermediary for questions large and small, without whom we would not have been able to experience the touching moments of the last inhabited lighthouses.

Thanks also to:

Admiral Sir Michael Livesay	*NLB Chairman*
James Taylor	*NLB Chief executive*
Jack Ross	*NLB Operation Officer*
Gordon Johson	*Chief of Oban Depot*
Ronni Coupper	*Chief of Stromness Depot*
Captain David Davidson	*MV Pharos*
Alan Provan	*MV Pharos*
The team of	*MV Pharos*
Angus Hutchison	*Last Principal Keeper of Fair Isle South*

Keepers:
Frank Bremner, Jim Watt, Alistair Henderson, Duncan Leslie, Jim Bain, Stewart Taylor, Donald Micheal, James Mackay, Alan Tulloch, Alex Smith.

Sarah Swallow, Scotland's Lighthouse Museum, for the images of Dubh Artach on pages 22 and 41 from the Keith Allardyce collection.

The inhabitants of Fair Isle:

Calum Falconer	*Bond Helicopter Pilot*
Toni Taylor	*Bond Helicopter Pilot*

IRELAND

Very special thanks to David Bedlow, *the Marine Department Administration Manager,* our intermediary, who did everything possible to facilitate all of our exceptional encounters.

Thanks also to:

Mel Boyd	*Chief Executive*
Captain Kieran O'Higgins	*Deputy Inspector Superintendent*
Micheal Donnaly	*Rossavell Helipad*
Vincent Sweeney	*Blacksod Helipad*
Donal Holland	*Castletownbeer Helipad*

Attendants:
Sean Faherthy, Donal O'Sullivan, Donal Coyle, John Joseph Doherty, Noël Gaughan, Ciaran Powell, Dick O'Driscol, Tucks Tweedy.

Michael Hennessy	*Pilot of Irish Helicopter*
Micheal Conneely	*Pilot of Irish Helicopter*
Mr Brennan	*Dun Loaghaire Maritime Museum*

WALES AND CORNWALL

Breeda Wall Trinity House Communication, London
Karl Ree

Russell Strowncer	*Penzance Depot*
Commander Graham Edmonds	*Royal Navy Gibraltar*

Trinity House Technicians:
Lenny Astley, Phil Miucci, Paul Kneebone, Ken Taylor.

Captain Paul Longdon	*Bond Helicopter*
Michael Marlic-Smith	*Castle Air Helicopter*